STREAMS
of
MERCY

STREAMS
of
MERCY

RECEIVING AND
REFLECTING
GOD'S GRACE

MARK RUTLAND

VINE
BOOKS

SERVANT PUBLICATIONS
ANN ARBOR, MICHIGAN

Vine Books is an imprint of Servant Publications especially designed
to serve evangelical Christians.

Published by Servant Publications
P.O. Box 8617
Ann Arbor, Michigan 48107

Cover design: Left Coast Design, Portland, OR

   00 01 02   10 9 8 7 6 5 4

Printed in the United States of America
ISBN 0-89283-998-8

LIBRARY OF CONGRESS CATALOGING-IN-PUBLICATION DATA

Rutland, Mark.
Streams of Mercy : receiving and reflecting God's grace / Mark
Rutland.
     p.   cm.
Includes bibliographical references.
ISBN 0-89283-998-8 (alk. paper)
1. God—Mercy.   2. Christian Life.   I. Title.
BT153.M4R88   1999
231.7—dc21   98-32193
                                        CIP

For My Alison

Ever always and never sometimes

Contents

Acknowledgments

The Holy Ghost
Without whom no book has healing grace

Bert Ghezzi
Publisher, friend and encourager

Gordon Miller
Indefatigable, steadfast and faithful typist and assistant

Liz Heaney
Vigilant editor and wise in counsel

"The quality of mercy is not strain'd,
It droppeth as the gentle rain from heaven."

———

PORTIA
The Merchant of Venice

Introduction

One of the great comedy sequences of cinematic history is the exchange between King Arthur and God in Monty Python's insane treatment of the Holy Grail.

"I will send you on a quest," God announces.

"Good idea, O Lord," Arthur beams.

"Of course it's a good idea!" God thunders.

All of God's ideas are good ones, and mercy is one of his best. A book on mercy was Bert Ghezzi's idea, and I believe that was also a good idea. Having me write it may not have been Bert's best thought yet, but I'm glad I got the opportunity, if for no other reason than it made me think more about the truly wonderful mercies of God in my own life.

When I was down for the count, God's mercies lifted me out of the miry clay and set my feet on a broad place. The mercy of God is not theory to me, but the rock under my feet.

Writing this book also made me think about what I perceive to be, by and large, a joyless and angry landscape in the American church. A couple of decades of American Christian subculture finding its motivational resource in a catalogue of socio-political causes has soured the sweet countenance of the Bride of Christ. Nothing in this book should be understood as an attack on those issues so dear to many of us, but the deep longing of one who aches to see Christianity smile, and even laugh, again.

In this book I don't want to explore the theological implications of mercy as an idea; instead I want to inspire a disheartened church to remember the mercies of God, and then show them to the world, to each other and, yes, to ourselves. I want to remind the church that there is a balm in Gilead that can make the wounded whole and happy and eager to apply that soothing salve to the wounds of others.

Streams of Mercy is divided into three sections: Part One is a catalogue of the mercies of God toward us. We need to remember just how marvelous are those "streams of mercy never ceasing," and that they do indeed "call for songs of loudest praise." What must follow does in Parts Two and Three: God's mercy to us, freshly rediscovered, flows out from us in our relationships and in the church.

I have written a short story that ties in to each chapter. This piece appears as a sidebar toward the end of each chapter. Any similarity to actual persons or events is purely coincidental. The purpose of these stories is to be thought-provoking rather than to actually illustrate the chapter. I hope you enjoy chewing on the stories *and* the chapters.

I pray you find in this book something to think about, something to make you laugh again and something to share with an old friend over a good cup of coffee and a cinnamon bun.

Mark Rutland

One

The Mercy We Need

I sat by the hospital bed of an angry homosexual who was dying of AIDS. He was a nineteen-year-old Hispanic, wearing a frilly, pink negligee and holding a teddy bear.

"I guess you came to tell me God hates gays," he said.

"No. I was afraid that's what you thought. I came to tell you God loves gays."

"I'm nearly twenty," he spat out. "I've had several thousand men as lovers since I was twelve. You mean God's not mad about that?"

"He's not mad. He's sad. You gave yourself AIDS, and your Creator is so very sad."

"Well, you're a strange preacher," he said, tears of frustration brimming in his eyes.

"Am I? In what way?"

"Well, don't you think sodomy is a sin?"

"Yes, I certainly do. Just like adultery and fornication and murder and stealing are sins. But I also know God still loves you. He's no more horrified at your sins than he is by mine."

We talked for about an hour before he prayed with me to confess his sins and trust in Christ as his Savior. When we looked up at each other from that prayer, he immediately asked for an orderly.

"Please," he said. "Tell him to hurry. I don't want to die in a pink nightgown."

A few hours later, that young man died in a plain green hospital gown. Just before he died, he whispered to me, "At my funeral, there'll be a lot of gays. Preach …" His voice trailed off.

"What?" I urged him. "Preach on what?"

"Mercy."

IN SEARCH OF MERCY

Mercy is one of those baseball and apple pie words. Everybody likes the sound of it. But some of its meanings have been lost, and others have been marred beyond recognition. We live in a generation that is careening between law and lawlessness. If there has ever been a people who need a fresh word of mercy, it's Americans at the turn of the millennium.

The modern United States citizen seems to believe that "suckered are the merciful, for they shall be railroaded." Indeed, mercy has fallen from its traditional status as a virtue, to become an antique that is prohibitively expensive and far too fragile for life in the fast lane. We have become a merciless people whose children—in extreme cases—use guns to settle arguments at school. We carry an angry ache for revenge. Los Angeles is still rebuilding from its riots, and the scene of Reginald Denny's pitiless beating haunts us yet. The rubble of the federal building in Oklahoma City is a monument to mercilessness. What kind of a monster, we ask ourselves, would kill so many?

Mothers slay their unborn without a backward glance, and the church cries for mercy. Then someone bombs an abortion clinic in the name of Christ and leaves behind a second antipersonnel device designed to kill and maim as many firemen and police as possible. This from a follower of the One who proclaimed that the merciful are blessed?

Mercy. It sounds good, but what does it mean, and how do I give it?

I am increasingly persuaded that the modern church is in danger of becoming a cold, unloving and humorless mockery of what God had in mind when Jesus preached his Sermon on the Mount and delivered the life-giving message, "Blessed are the merciful." Jesus came to reveal a God of mercy, to make his children merciful and to plant in this sad, angry, hurting world a church motivated by mercy.

Yet the world accuses God of being merciless. And who can blame them? A merciless church, filled with merciless lives, preaches a merciful God. If the tables were turned, wouldn't you have a hard time believing the gospel message?

I once shared an elevator in a Houston hotel with a man whose features were a portrait of discouraged fatigue. He slumped lifelessly against the wall, his face as gray as his overcoat.

"Are you all right?" I asked.

"School board," he muttered, as if this explained everything.

"Ahh," I said. "Rough meeting?"

"The Christians came today," he responded, and I

thought he said the word *Christians* the way Christians used to say *lions*.

"Was it that bad?"

He shrugged. "Oh, no worse than they usually are. Placards, yelling, rudeness, interruptions. You know. It's just that my mother is dying in Dallas, and today I guess the Christians were just too much for me."

REMEMBERING THE MERCIES OF GOD

If the merciful are as blessed as Jesus says, then Christians just may be in the soup. We need a fresh look at mercy. But where do we look?

"It is because of the Lord's mercies that we are not consumed, because his compassions fail not. They are new every morning; great is thy faithfulness" (Lamentations 3:22-23). Perhaps by looking at the mercies of God, we can refresh our memories about who we are called to be as individual Christians, and then see what that might look like together, as the church in the world.

Franky Schaeffer wrote *A Time for Anger* and therein made a good, solid case for righteous indignation. Certainly to everything, even anger, there is a season, but right now our poor angry world—full of angry people, living in angry families—needs the sweet savor of mercy. Where will that come from if not from a merciful church, full of merciful people, serving a merciful God?

MERCY OR GRACE?

Now, what is mercy? I think you know. If a convicted felon "throws himself on the mercy of the court," he does not expect the judge to say, "I have no idea what you mean." The judge may say, "There is no mercy for you." Or he may even grant mercy, but he will most certainly not ask for an explanation.

For theological purposes, many people love to make much over the distinction between mercy and grace. The common pastoral explanation is that grace gives that which we do not deserve, while mercy withholds the punishment we do deserve. But in real life such fineness in thought breaks down.

If a medical missionary doctor treats a dying leper, do we call the doctor's action grace or mercy? Grace, perhaps, if we can convince ourselves that the leper does not deserve to be helped. But then, who does? Or is it mercy, because the leper deserves to die? That conclusion depends on our ability to convince ourselves that the leper's condition is his well-earned punishment. Either way, it will not matter to the leper. "Have mercy, have mercy!" he cries. And someone moved by the grace of God offers help.

When Jesus came to earth, he came on a mission of mercy. Or was it grace? We are saved by grace because God is merciful. He shows us mercy because he is full of grace.

I am not attempting to blur whatever distinction the catechisms make. It's just that I don't choose to make them here, because I don't think they will help anyone to believe in the mercies of God or to live them out.

So, you may ask, is this book about mercy or is it about grace? My answer is, yes.

That begs several questions. Do we need the mercy of God? Why? If I am to preach on mercy at the funerals of people who have died from AIDS, I want to know first if there is any—for them *and* for me.

GETTING WHAT WE DESERVE

Once we face what we are really like, we will never again doubt our need for mercy. The Old Testament documents the human condition in all its fallenness. Shakespeare said, "All's well that ends well." That being true, the Old Testament is a case study in a humanity that is not well and is well in need of mercy. Genesis starts with a front-row view on creation and ends at a graveside. The Old Testament itself begins with the blessing of creation and ends with a curse on the earth.

In the beginning God ... are the four most hope-filled words in literature. The Book of Genesis begins with promise and no hint at all of what lies ahead. Imagine the dawn of the virginal day, fresh and pure and gleaming in the clean light of a newborn sun. Listen to the trill of the meadowlark singing her primal melody, and behold the mighty whale's first breach to burst through the sparkling azure surface of a pristine, unsailed sea. But before the first book of the Bible ends, murder, war, wickedness and perversion have stained every page.

I remember years ago I went to see Dino De Laurentiis'

movie *The Bible*, which of course covers only a few portions of Genesis. When the movie was over and the lights came on, a woman directly behind me turned to her little daughter and observed, "I don't think that's the whole story."

Certainly it is not. There's much worse stuff in Genesis than Hollywood in the early sixties dared to put on the screen. De Laurentiis left out some stories so sordid that I have seldom if ever heard them even approached in a sermon. For example, the story of Judah's tryst with a roadside prostitute who turns out to be his daughter-in-law (see Genesis 38). We read of Lot, who impregnated both of his own daughters in two drunken, incestuous nights in a cave (see Genesis 19). And then there's Noah, whose first noble act following the flood was to get drunk and accidentally expose himself to his own son whom he then cursed for peeking (see Genesis 9:20-23). Don't forget Abraham's cowardly willingness to share his wife rather than be killed for her sake—twice! (see Genesis 12 and 20). Nor should we leave out Joseph's brothers, who sold him into slavery (see Genesis 37:28); Jacob, who cheated his brother (see Genesis 27:19); or Sarah, who put her Egyptian handmaiden and an innocent little boy out in the desert to die (see Genesis 21:10).

Genesis stretches from Eden's garden of bliss to the desert's slavery and death. The Genesis account never flinches to report the truth about fallen humanity. The same is true of the whole Old Testament. The rebellion, idolatry, witchcraft, suicide, mass murder and incestuous rape among David's descendants alone is staggering. Israel's royal line was more debauched than the notorious members of the modern House of Windsor. And the population was hardly nobler. They rejected and murdered the prophets, worshiped false gods and occasionally resorted to human sacrifice. Is it any wonder, then, that the Old Testament ends with the words "smite the earth with a curse"?

After all the kings and prophets paraded across the stage of history from Exodus to Malachi, the curse that infested the ground in Genesis remained. Death had come into the earth as a curse, and no one could remove it—not Moses, not Abraham, not Isaiah nor any of the prophets. Nothing could. Not even the Law made a difference. In fact, the Law gave the curse its strength. Not that the Law was bad. How could the law of a good God be bad? But an immutable law written on tablets of stone hung like the sword of Damocles over the heads of an outlaw race. Cursed by its own sin and judged worthy of death by the Law it broke, the world lay in darkness, from Adam to Malachi. Occasional flickers of hope came: the Psalms, the prophets, the sacrifices—first in the tabernacle and then in the temple. Then after Malachi, silence for four hundred years!

From the pure, sweet light of the dawn of creation, humanity descended the slippery steps of rebellion downward, ever downward, into a pit as dark as midnight and as silent as death. What the sons and daughters of Adam *deserved* was a coffin in Egypt. What we *deserve* is death. But, oh, what we need is mercy!

COMPLICATED MERCY

Most everyone agrees that we need mercy. But we want a narrow mercy, not an incarnate God's wide mercy. Many Christians resort to one of two extremes—either the law or all slates wiped clean. Those of a religious bent want a "just" God who will kick the sinners into hell with a loud harumph and lead the righteous (themselves) to pillows in heaven. Libertines want a "God of grace" who will level the playing field the other way around. Their gentle old grandpa in the sky excuses everything, forgives all, remembers nothing and universally cleanses. Humankind hopes to force God into a human justice as carnal and rigid as its own.

Divine mercy, however, is not so simple. If we demand that God be either *always* forgiving (universalism), or that he "give us what we deserve" (religious pride), we will lose sight of the marvelous divine mercy that comforts the troubled, then troubles the comfortable.

All Jesus' stories reveal a God of mercy who was not at all to the liking of legalistic Pharisees. But after shocking them with a story of grace and mercy, Jesus would turn right around and give a description of hell lurid enough to curl the hair of any self-respecting liberal. *Why, he acts as though he doesn't care if he pleases any of us!*

Take, for example, the story of Lazarus the beggar (see Luke 16). That is an equal opportunity parable; it contains something offensive for everyone. First of all, it tells of a flaming hell and a man suffering there for his sins. That puts a damper on universalism's Pollyanna attitude toward judgment. But for legalists, the wrong guy is in the flames! Lazarus is given heaven as a reward for poverty. The rich man, whom some might assume was walking in blessings—because he had tithed, refused to cosign notes and invested wisely—goes to hell. What? Are we to assume from this parable that God will bless us with merited prosperity, then curse us with unmerited hell? If the rich man was evil, why was he rich? And if he was a good man, why was he in hell? If Lazarus was a wicked enough steward to be poor, then why was he in heaven?

The Pharisees and the liberals hated that story when Jesus told it, and they still do. They think, *No siree, Bob, this crazy parable is altogether too complicated. Now, if you put the poor man in hell, there is at least a good moral lesson on the final consequences of disordered living; poverty now and hell to pay later. That makes sense. Furthermore, with the rich man in the bosom of Abraham, the lesson is doubly learned. Follow biblical principles and enjoy the meat and potatoes of prosperity in the present, and pie in the sky for dessert. Now, that's a story worth telling! The Lazarus thing won't work at all.*

But what if we've missed the point? What if the story is about mercy instead of money? Let me explain. When the rich man cries out from hell's flames, he pleads for mercy. That is not so surprising; but the fact that he ties that mercy to the person of Lazarus is amazing. "Father Abraham," he cried, "have mercy on me, and send Lazarus, that he may dip the tip of his finger in water, and cool my tongue; for I am tormented in this flame" (Luke 16:24).

Why Lazarus? Heaven is full of saints and angels. Why Lazarus, indeed. It must be that the rich man had identified the beggar at his gate as a man likely to undertake a mission of mercy straight into the fires of Gehenna. Lazarus must have been known as a forgiving man, or the rich man would have said, "Send anyone but Lazarus. He'll dry his finger off before he gets here."

Instead he says, "I can see heaven with all its hosts. They may all be fine, but Lazarus' life was lived before my very eyes. I know him to be a man of grace and mercy. I know *he* will come. He will help me, even if I refused to help him. I know he will."

There may be even more here. If poor Lazarus went to heaven because he was merciful, then maybe the rich man was damned for lack of it. When he saw Lazarus in Abraham's arms, was the rich man's conscience quick to recall his own merciless, judgmental selfishness? Did he remember turning his face away from the beggar at his gate? Was his calloused, merciless soul able to remember each time he had laid the blame for Lazarus' affliction and poverty on the poor man himself? "Look, children, look at that beggar. That is what will become of you if you do not love God, invest wisely and go to the right schools. That man has caused his own poverty. Now he wants to cause ours. He did not earn money, but he wants me to give him what I've earned. 'Will work for food.' Hah! That's a laugh."

The story of Lazarus and the rich man confuses many of us. We want to believe that rich people deserve to be rich. How can they deserve hell at the same time? The Scripture says that the seed of the righteous never have to beg for bread (see Psalm 37:25). Yet Lazarus did. If Lazarus is righteous, why is he begging for bread? What does that verse mean, if not what it appears to mean?

The problem here must be God, because he is the one who decides these things. Perhaps Jesus was trying to tell us something in the story of the beggar who goes to heaven and a rich man who goes to hell. It must be about God. But what? Whatever it was, we're not sure we like it.

MERCY FOUND ON THE WAY FROM MALACHI TO MATTHEW

We're also not sure we like the point of the Prodigal Son story in Luke 15. It presents the same problematic view of God's values. From the way he told the story, it's clear that Jesus wants us to think the elder brother is the bad guy. Why? Does that mean the younger brother is the good guy? No! The younger brother—the one who runs away—is also a bad guy.

The only good guy in the parable is the father, and his treatment of the prodigal makes no sense. A warm welcome, full acceptance, merciful forgiveness and a fiesta make for an odd sense of justice. In our minds the young rebel should have been sent back to the pigpen he put himself in. After all, the boy squandered his inheritance and his own potential. If it's a coffin in Egypt he wants, let him have one. After all, he made his bed! The worthless boy began with a blessing and ended in a pigsty. That's surely the earth with a curse, and if anybody ever deserved it....

But, by the mercies of God, the close of one covenant

is the beginning of another. Turn the page at the end of Malachi and leap across four hundred years of silence into a new beginning, a whole new generation. *This is the generation of Jesus.* A new day had dawned. So when the prodigal staggered into his father's arms, still stinking of pigs, he found a new birth. He was suddenly part of a new generation that did not live under the guilt and condemnation of squandered potential but in the tender embrace of a fresh beginning. The boy got up out of the pig filth, foully cursed by his own sin, and in one homeward journey walked all the way from Malachi to Matthew. There, he found mercy.

The father in Jesus' stories was his own, whom he knew to be a God of tender but complicated mercies. Jesus knew that in heaven's view, repentance covered with pig filth is holy, but religious ostentation and proud legalism are no more than manure.

This God was not the god of the Pharisees of Jesus' day, and he still isn't today. Pharisees want the divine payoff: the rich should get richer, and to hell with the poor. Pharisees want a god of rules for everything—rules for heaven, for healing and for hell itself. They want a God as horrified at humanity as they are.

Instead, Jesus reveals a loving Father whose joyous laughter booms from heaven's porch, who deliriously dances in the dust as up the road comes a wicked, wicked boy with pig manure on his feet and tears in his eyes. Such a God saw a creation so under the curse that all he could do was crawl under it with them and nail the rules, all the rules, to himself. That kind of God would never stand off to the side, disinterested and sullen. That kind of God would never just give up on us. Neither will he just excuse us. But he will die for us.

On the cross, a merciful God offered us grace out of his great love. Love, grace and mercy all mingled sweetly there.

The Old Testament starts with creation and ends with death, the grave and a curse. But that's not God's final word on the subject. Maybe Shakespeare was right that it's the ending that counts. But Malachi was not the end. Every epistle in the New Testament from Romans to Hebrews ends with grace. Repetition for slow learners can also be an act of mercy. Then, as if God wanted to make sure we didn't miss it, the last sentence of Revelation is, "The grace of our Lord Jesus Christ be with you all."

"Now, Lord, do you mean mercy or grace?" we ask.

"Yes," comes the answer from heaven. "I do."

What about the grave at the end of Genesis? Defeated! And the curse at the end of Malachi? Broken! And Adam and Eve? Forgiven, redeemed and adopted! Our God is a God of mercy. All his thoughts toward us are merciful. He has been telling us that from the beginning.

If we could only hear of his mercies, maybe we would learn to love again, and to laugh at ourselves, and to rejoice. Having been shown a lot of mercy by a God of perfect holiness, perhaps, we could manage, once again, to cut each other a little slack. And maybe, just maybe, we could even find enough mercy to cut ourselves a little slack and, hey, lighten up!

When God, in the famous burning bush appearance, sent Moses down into Egypt to lead the Hebrew slaves to freedom, Moses asked an unusual question. He said,

"When I come unto the children of Israel, and shall say unto them, The God of your fathers hath sent me unto you; and they shall say to me, What is his name? what shall I say unto them?" (Exodus 3:13).

It is striking that Moses did not make the request for Egypt's sake. Israel needed a fresh revelation of God. Even so, the Western church needs a reminder every now and again of the sweet mercies of God. My sincerest prayer is a simple one, and the motivation for this book. I pray that you will see, as never before, that our God is not the cosmic cop, not the angry, absentee landlord who is out to catch you in your mischief, but a fountain of mercy full and free. Then having seen anew that river, I pray that you might be refreshed for merciful living and merciful churchmanship.

The Odor of the Condemned

Jerry was ashamed. He had never been so ashamed in his life. He wished he were dead. He would gladly die now, right now, here on this bench, and let them find his body and take it home to his parents. He would much rather die than face Sister Margarite.

He wished he would just die. He sat looking at his shoes and avoiding the eyes of other kids as they passed him in the hall. None of them knew for sure what he had done, but all kids know the look of another kid in trouble. They can smell the odor of the condemned.

He was not afraid of Sister Margarite, but he dreaded seeing her face. He liked the jolly nun. She was a good principal, always laughing and teasing the kids in the hall. Everybody liked her except the chronically misbehaved. Jerry was not one of those. He was usually a quiet, shy boy who was serious about the sixth grade. But this! More hot tears of shame stung his eyes, and sixth-grade girls passing quietly in the hall looked at him with what he was certain was disgust. Maybe they despised him for being the kind of weakling who sat on the bench in the hall outside the principal's office and cried like a baby. Or perhaps they knew about the magazines hidden in his locker. He wished he would die.

"Jerry," Sister Margarite's voice said, and he jumped like he had been shot. "You can come in now."

He got up from the bench and walked past her without saying a word or looking at her. There was a chair in front of her desk and he stood beside it with his hand on the arm.

"Sit down, Jerry," she said. "I've called you in to help me with something."

He lifted his eyes slowly, barely daring to hope. Maybe there had been a mix-up. Maybe the teacher had thrown the magazines away and sent him to the office to trick him. Maybe …

"Jerry, you see this?" the moon-faced nun asked, indicating an ancient tape player on her desk.

"Yes, Ma'am."

"It drags."

"Uh-huh."

"You know, the music drags."

"Uh-huh."

"Well," she said brightly. "They tell me you know about these things. Do you? What's wrong with it?"

He gaped at her. Was this happening? Relief began to flood into him.

"The heads need cleaning," he said, his voice barely above a whisper. "I can clean them for you."

"Oh!" she exclaimed and clapped her chubby little hands in delight. "They told me you were just the boy. I guess they were right. How long will it take?"

"I'll bring it back tomorrow."

"Good, good, good," she said, stuffing the massive boom box into his arms and pushing him toward the door. "That'll be great."

It was over. He'd made it. He couldn't believe his luck. He wanted to dance. He just put his hand to the doorknob when she spoke to him casually, softly.

"I know you're wondering, Jerry. I threw those magazines away. Look, Jerry, all little boys are curious about women's bodies. That's how God keeps the human race going. Someday you'll find all that out. But not now, Jerry."

He turned to look directly into her pale blue eyes. "I'm sorry, Sister," he said. "I'm really sorry."

"And I'm sorry about your mom. You must be lonely without her."

"Yes, Ma'am."

"Did you know that my mother died when I was only eight?"

"No, Ma'am."

"Tomorrow, when you bring back my player, we'll talk about it."

"OK."

"And, Jerry ..."

"Yes, Ma'am?"

"Let's not ever mention those magazines again."

"If you say so," he whispered.

"I say so. I love you, Jerry."

"I love you, too, Sister."

*"It is because of the Lord's mercies
that we are not consumed."*

LAMENTATIONS 3:22

Two

Mercy's Price Tag

Once, a small boy asked me why we call Good Friday "good."

"Well," I explained, "it's because that's the day Jesus died."

"What's good about that?" he asked.

Good question. Even the best news is usually bad for somebody. Thanksgiving is a family feast full of great joy for all. All but the turkey, that is. Across the hall from the riotous celebration in the winner's locker room, sad-faced losers lap up the dregs of defeat. Rocky dances triumphantly around the ring, shouting his indomitable "Yo, Adrian, I did it!" But in the far corner, Apollo Creed lies flat on his back, trying to breathe in enough smelling salts to make sense of the ceiling lights.

When the Prodigal Son returned, the father and his faithful servants saw it as the best news imaginable. The older brother sulked because he knew he would have to relinquish or at least share the title of "good son." Deep in his heart he knew that it was good news, but self-interest and hidden agendas stole his joy. We have to remember that half the family fortune had been squandered by his vagabond sibling now being welcomed so joyfully. The elder "good son" had to face the reality that the remaining half, his half, would now be cut in half again. That was not good news to him. Perhaps it should have been, but it wasn't. For beyond whatever financial concerns may have plagued the elder son, an even more reprehensible motive gnawed away at the joy he might have had.

The spiritual jealousy and righteous indignation of those merciless saints of sanctimony is a barrier to grace. The elder brother was just plain angry because his prodigal sibling got a fiesta instead of a flogging. The issue was the conflict between justice and mercy.

Self-pity, self-congratulation, self-absorption and a host of other hyphenated sins erode mercy in angry, sullen waves that pound remorselessly against the coastline of Christian charity. The smug and self-righteous always sulk when sinners avoid their comeuppance. The elder brother's outraged sense of justice silenced his brotherly love and shut him out of his father's full joy.

Still, there's one character in the story for whom the return of the prodigal really meant bad news. No hidden agenda, no ugly veiled self-interest, just plain bad news. The fatted calf viewed the return of the dear wayward boy with a jaundiced eye. This was going to be a great party with a terrific barbecue. Whether that's good news or bad news depends on whether you're a chef or a calf.

Without the shedding of blood there is no remission of sins, says Hebrews 9:22. That one sentence captures the double edge of Christ's mercy. On the one hand, there is remission of sins. That is the great, good news for us who need mercy so badly. But the shedding of blood is not a happy prospect for the one whose blood is shed. If we are to rediscover mercy, we need to know, first of all, what mercy cost and who paid the price.

In the tabernacle of Moses, in the Holy of Holies, in the ark of the covenant lay the two stone tables of immutable law that hopelessly condemned all of humanity. Above those commandments was a flat covering called the judgment seat. Two winged cherubim peered down upon it from either side, and their gaze signified that our sins were ever before God's ceaseless, sleepless, sinless eyes.

Once a year, on the tenth of Tishri, the high priest would enter this holiest place and sprinkle blood upon that awesome seat of judgment. Those precious atoning drops turned judgment into mercy because the eyes of heaven cannot see through blood.

Jesus himself made reference to the mercy seat in his biting story of the two men who prayed in the temple. Jesus treated the first man with bitter sarcasm, harshly mocking his smug, unrepentant religiosity. But into the mouth of the humbler, more penitent sinner, Jesus put these words, "God, be merciful to me a sinner," or as it may be read more literally, "God, be mercy-seated to me a sinner" (Luke 18:9-14).

How odd that in a story about the mercy seat, Jesus treats the first man so mercilessly. Why use such a negative example? First of all, for contrast's sake. The purpose of all dark background in creative expression is to make the light more apparent. More importantly, Jesus wanted to be clear on the dangers of despising divine mercy. We cannot have it both ways. We are either hopeless sinners, covered by the blood, or we must stand naked before the judgment seat. Only by the shedding of blood is there remission of sin, and that blood must be unalloyed with our "righteousness," which is never more than religious posturing.

God views us either with judgment or with mercy. The blood makes the difference. Broken by our sinfulness, making our humble confession and trusting in the blood, we find atonement. Proud, self-righteous and trusting in our own goodness, we manage only to pry the lid off the bloodstained mercy seat. When we do, we expose the ministry of death contained in the Law.

When the men of Beth-shemesh looked inside the ark, more than fifty thousand people died (1 Samuel 6:19-20). Unless our sins are covered by the blood, we will likewise perish. Look into the Law and die, but let God behold the blood, and judgment turns to mercy.

Such great mercy is only available by the shedding of blood—Christ's blood.

> There is a fountain filled with blood
>> Drawn from Emmanuel's veins,
> And sinners, plunged beneath that flood,
>> Lose all their guilty stains.[1]

Mercy cost me nothing, but it cost God death on a cross. Having paid so great a price for my redemption, God leaves the choosing or rejecting of it up to me. I can be washed in the blood, but there is no mercy for the proud.

> The dying thief rejoiced to see
>> That fountain in his day;
> And there may I, though vile as he,
>> Wash all my sins away.[2]

THE ATTITUDE OF MERCY

The wonderful mercy of Christ's sacrificial love is revealed not just in what he did but in how he did it. We know that he died for our sins. We are usually less aware, and less grateful, that Christ is no whining martyr, wallowing in self-pity.

After his resurrection, Jesus met the disciples in Galilee, where they had gone to fish and recover from their woundedness. They had failed their Lord, disappointed themselves, disillusioned each other and had almost abandoned the hopes and dreams Jesus had implanted in them. He was dead, and they had returned to their fishing boats.

Their reunion is recorded in John 21. As they drag themselves and their fish onto the rocky shoreline, Jesus stands to greet them lovingly. Behind him a cozy fire beckons with the smell of food cooking over glowing coals. The scene astounds them. The risen Lord is alone. Has he caught and cleaned these fish? Did he build this fire, slice the bread and cook for *them?* Once before he washed their feet. Now, will he cook for them? They are not sure.

"Come and dine," Jesus says at last (John 21:12).

Their hearts leap. He does not stand, tapping his foot impatiently, and scold them as they deserve. He does not remind them of their failures or of his sacrifice. He simply says, "Come and dine." His invitation is filled with mercy. He invites them to eat mercy and warm themselves by the glowing embers of a merciful fire.

As Peter approaches timidly and stretches his cold, wet

hands to the fire, his eyes meet Jesus'. In Peter's eyes is the agony of an unspeakable apology. In Jesus' eyes there is something Peter cannot at first identify. What is it that he sees? Then Peter looks down at the fire. Something about this seems familiar. When was the last time he warmed his hands at a fire? Suddenly the memory bursts clear upon his mind. *Oh, no!* Peter recoils, remembering. He warmed his hands just like this on the night he denied Jesus with a curse. Involuntarily, almost against his will, Peter jerks away his hand, and his eyes lift from the fire to Jesus' face. Oh, those eyes! Peter longs to look away and cannot.

There it is again. What does he see in Jesus' eyes? He has seen it before. The woman taken in adultery darts through his mind. Why would he think of her at a time like this? Is that a smile at the corner of Jesus' mouth?

Suddenly Peter knows what it is, that unidentifiable inner flame that warms the Master's eyes. Mercy! The bread, the fish, the scene, even the charcoal fire—all announce in perfect harmony the wonderful answer to Peter's "unspeakable apology." What Peter longs to do is run to Jesus, to weep on his shoulder and tell him, "I'm sorry! I lied. I denied. I cursed. What can I—?"

But before he ever says it, the answer is in Jesus' eyes and in the glowing charcoal and in the Master's voice. "Look. See the food. All is forgiven. Let's eat together."

COME AND DINE

Some years ago, I read of a survey in which thousands of Americans were asked what they would most like to hear said to them. The top three responses were listed. I guessed the most popular one, but I was flabbergasted at numbers two and three.

Number 1 was the fairly predictable, "I love you."

Number 2 was, "I forgive you." When I read that, I remembered one pathetic scene in Hemingway's *Islands in the Stream*. The protagonist, having wasted and lost much—his wife, his life, his son—stands with a male servant at the end of a lonely rock jetty. Staring out at the sea, he says, "I feel like I ought to apologize. And for the life of me I can't think who to."[3]

We long to hear that we are forgiven, but for the life of us we can't think of the one who can say it.

Number 3 was the shocker. I laughed to discover that the third most popular phrase with Americans was, "Supper's ready."

Then it dawned on me. That's the whole gospel! Jesus stands behind the communion table with his nail-scarred hands outstretched and the light of sacrificial mercy in his eyes. His voice, his words meet us with healing warmth as we drag our water-logged burdens up the rocky shoreline from life's most chilling seas.

"I love you," he whispers. "I forgive you. Come and dine."

Come and dine, the Master calleth, come and dine!
You may feast at Jesus' table all the time.

He who fed the multitudes, turned the water into
  wine,
To the hungry calleth now, "Come and dine."[4]

For the sinful to sit and be filled, the innocent must
always pay the price. The fatted calf paid the supreme
price for the Prodigal Son's homecoming feast. The Angel
of Death passed over every house in Goshen that had
lamb's blood smeared on the door. That was fine for the
Jews inside, but not so great for the lamb. Abraham
untied Isaac's hands and saw a ram caught by his horns in
a bramble bush. God had indeed, as Abraham prophe-
sied, supplied a sacrifice. Isaac was spared. But the ram
had to die.

On Yom Kippur, when the High Priest poured out the
blood of atonement upon that golden stool by sacrifice,
the innocent died for the damned, and the judgment seat
became the mercy seat. They are one and the same place.
God is just, and his justice cannot simply be set aside
with a kindly wink at sin. No, he says, sin means the punishment of death. And someone must die. But, he hastens
to add, let it be me. My blood, my sacrifice turns the place
of judgment into the mercy seat. When the blood was
applied, the judgment seat in the tabernacle became the
mercy seat, and today Calvary is the mercy seat for the
whole world.

Good Friday is good, after all.

The Foxhole

The four of them lay in the mud and in their own hatred. Ortega, who had volunteered for service in Vietnam, was next to Butler, who despised the white military-industrial establishment for sending poor blacks to die in the jungle while they got rich on napalm contracts. On the other side of the hole were Marchiloni, the brooding Italian draftee from New York, and Witherspoon, whose wife had served him with divorce papers the day the Tet Offensive began. They glared at each other but said nothing.

What was there to say? They were surrounded, cut off, and it was raining too hard for the choppers to get in. Morning was a long way off. None of the four had high hopes of being alive when the sun came up.

Witherspoon stretched his left leg toward Butler, sending a small tidal wave of muddy water sloshing across the black man's boots. Their eyes met and Butler let all his hatred show. Witherspoon's eyes showed nothing.

"Keep still, you moron," Butler snarled. "Look what you've done."

Witherspoon said nothing, but he calmly lowered the barrel of his weapon until it was pointing directly at Butler's chest.

The bookish, professional white man remained expressionless, but Ortega was certain that if Butler made a single threatening move, Witherspoon would shoot. *Probably just clean his rifle and never say a word,* Ortega thought.

When the big black man snorted, turning his back on Witherspoon, Marchiloni chuckled bitterly, but Witherspoon still showed no emotion.

He's crazy, Ortega thought. *His wife done drove him crazy. What am I saying? Witherspoon ain't the only one. We're all crazy. I'm crazy, too. I came here to fight for my country, and I'm as nuts as Witherspoon. I'd just as soon kill Butler or Marchiloni or Witherspoon as I would Charlie. It ain't raining water, it's raining hate—insane, murdering hate—and I'm as wet as everybody else.*

"I'm coming in," said a voice in the darkness, and the four weapon bolts shot like a metallic symphony. "It's Chaplain Wang. Shoot a chaplain and God gets real mad."

With that, the familiar figure of the chaplain slid down into their wet abode. Wang was a Chinese-American from San Francisco who had left a sizable Catholic church to come to Nam. He was jovial, full of encouragement and popular with the men.

"Hey," Wang grinned. "Nice place you got here."

"Yeah," Marchiloni snapped. "Five-star."

"Ah, and a joy to me it is to see a fellow Catholic so bright and cheery under such circumstances," Wang said in an excellent Irish accent.

The incongruity of a Chinese priest speaking in an Irish accent brought a reluctant smile to Butler's face, and despite his intent to hide it from the chaplain, Wang's eyes caught the grin.

"Now let's see here," Wang said, switching easily to a Southern good ol' boy accent. "Ain't this here a sitiation? We got a I-talian Catholic from some place up North, a Mexican Catholic from Texas, a white Lutheran from Minnesota and a black Baptist from Talladega. Join the army an' see the world, that's what I say. Don't rain like this in Talladega, does it Butler?"

Butler grinned in spite of himself. He had to admit it. This priest could do accents better than most TV comedians. Wang sounded just like every dumb cracker white boy in his home state of Alabama. What amazed Butler the most was Wang's ability to remember the names of individual soldiers and every bit of information they had ever told him.

"Well," Wang said, returning to his own flat California accent, "looks like a long night. Anybody need a prayer?"

"Move on, priest," Witherspoon muttered darkly. "This isn't a praying hole. This is Satan's hole."

Ortega glanced at Witherspoon. It was the most he had ever heard the Midwesterner say. Witherspoon was nuts all right. But he was also right. This hole was no place for a priest, especially a nice guy like Father Wang.

Before Ortega could open his mouth to encourage the kindly priest to move along, the dull, deadly thunk of a grenade in the mud propelled all five men into action.

"Grenade!" Butler screamed, and even in the terror of the moment Ortega noticed how high-pitched and shrill the big man's voice was. Maybe fear makes women of all men. Ortega heard Marchiloni cursing as he dropped his weapon and clawed his way up the muddy embankment.

"Everybody out!" shouted Wang.

Ortega watched as the priest hurled himself into the murky darkness at their feet. Then the hole erupted in a mind-stunning, blinding flash that threw the Lutheran from Minnesota nearly twelve feet, blinded Marchiloni in one eye and gave Butler a concussion. Of the four, Ortega's wounds were the bloodiest, but even shrapnel wounds heal eventually. The priest was dead; his body lay over the grenade. Wang had taken the full explosion and almost certainly spared the lives of the four soldiers.

The priest's personal effects and a Silver Star were sent to his mother in San Francisco. Ortega, who spent twelve weeks in a hospital in Germany, kept telling himself that he would write to her, but he never did.

Ortega was amazed when Witherspoon visited him. Walking with a cane, the Midwesterner looked old and sad, but the craziness in his eyes was missing. He stood by the side of the bed and stared down at Ortega with an odd expression.

"You gonna be OK?" Witherspoon asked.

"Yeah, I'm going home," Ortega said. "Harlingen, Texas, is gonna look good to me."

"Yeah," Witherspoon responded without emotion. "I'm going home, too. Minneapolis. The limp is permanent, they say."

"Sorry," Ortega muttered, unsure of what to say.

"Yeah, me too. Listen, Ortega, I want to ask you something. How come he did that? What do *you* think?"

"Who ... Wang? Who knows? Impulse maybe."

"But why?" Witherspoon asked rather intensely. "Why Wang? He was the only one of us who should have lived, and he died. That ain't right."

Ortega glanced at the tiny silver crucifix that dangled from his bedpost. His grandmother had given it to him.

"No," Ortega agreed. "It ain't right. But it's the way it is. I think it's the way it's gotta be."

None of the four ever saw each other after that. Ortega always wondered whatever became of the others. He tried to go to college for a while, but it just didn't work for him. He finally went to work for a construction firm in McAllen and coached Little League. The boys loved him because he was the only coach they ever had who never yelled at them.

Three

God's Wide Mercy

One of the rabbinical tales portrays a surprising and disturbing conversation between God and Moses. In this story, God calls to Moses just as Miriam and the women begin to dance and sing on the sands of the Red Sea.

"Moses," God says, "what is this sound of tambourines?"

"The people are rejoicing, Lord," Moses explains. "The waters of the Red Sea have destroyed the Egyptian army, and the women are dancing."

"What? The work of my hands is drowned in the sea, and you rejoice?"

This story illustrates a great mystery. Mercy complicates everything. When we inspect the way we interpret and respond to history, a disturbing thought intrudes. If the mercies of God are shown at the cost of blood, who may receive them? Humankind has always had difficulty with that. Maybe we don't have God's point of view. Perhaps we do not even begin to understand how God thinks. Maybe we rejoice when we should weep, and weep when we ought to dance.

Such a God is confusing; we never know what to expect. We can deal with a withdrawn God. Let him be distant, uncaring and separated from our sins. That we understand. A cold stepfather in a not-too-blended home. Let him hide behind his newspaper and his busyness and his unapproachable macho shield. That is not news to us. In fact, we rather like the idea of an uninvolved God. We do not feel any need whatsoever to report in. *He's there? OK, I'm here. He doesn't need me and I don't need him. He's not mad at me, you say? That's because he doesn't even care enough to be angry.*

We can even understand an actively angry God. Of course he's angry. Why shouldn't he be? We have sinned and that's that. Now God's mad and our response to his anger is to give as good as we get. *He's angry? Hey, so am I! What about Rwanda and Bosnia? Let God explain natural disasters that wipe out whole towns, and the famine in Ethiopia, and then maybe I'll explain some things in my life. So God's mad? Congratulations. We're all mad! He doesn't come to my house, I don't go to his.*

Or perhaps God is concerned, loving and totally without law. *Hooray! Every altar call for my whole life has told me that "Just As I Am" is good enough for God.* But what does that mean? Is he then an indulgent old grandpa with enough of a bad past himself to put him in no mood to judge? A playful wink, a knowing shrug of his shoulders, because boys will be boys?

None of these images lines up with the big picture. Scripture depicts God as one who shows mercy *and* righteous judgment. Yes, Jesus comforted the woman taken in adultery. Indeed, he saved her life and refused to condemn her. But he also drove the money changers from the temple with a whip. I can see men screaming, coins flying and shocked faces, but I don't hear anyone singing

"Gentle Jesus, Meek and Mild." On the one hand, Christ forgave prostitutes and healed lepers; on the other hand, he called religious leaders snakes. He refused to use the word *adulteress* to a woman "caught in the act," but he was not reluctant to call people hypocrites, and he even called the Pharisees "whitewashed tombs ... full of dead men's bones" (Matthew 23:27, NIV). Jesus obviously had a different idea of mercy, at least of when and how to use it. He showed plenty of mercy to prostitutes, but resorted to bitter sarcasm and straight-out name-calling with the religious leaders of his nation.

A DIFFERENT KIND OF MERCY

A remarkable story in Luke 9 says much about Christ's view of mercy and ours. Jesus and his disciples were preaching their way from Caesarea to Jerusalem. As they approached each village, an advance team would go in and prepare the crowd to hear Jesus. Then the Master himself would arrive for the main meeting.

On this particular journey, Jesus' entourage decided to go through Samaria rather than around it, as most Jews would have done. Samaria was considered a polluted area populated by unclean half-castes whose lifestyles were corrupt and whose theology was heretical. Though they probably reckoned it another of Jesus' eccentricities, the disciples went along with his plan to preach in Samaria. I doubt they wanted to be there or that they cared about the Samaritans, but Jesus had done things like this before, and they must have decided to keep their mouths shut.

When the advance team from one village returned with a rebuff, however, it was the last straw for the disciples. They would not stand for some crummy Samaritan village rejecting Jesus—and them.

"Lord," said James and John, "shall we call down fire upon them like Elijah did? Please let us burn them up. Puh-lease, let us burn them!"

Jesus' answer stunned them. "The power that Elijah used was the Holy Spirit, who is within you as well. But you do not understand that Spirit or what it is he wants to do in you. You do not understand yourselves and you do not understand the Spirit. I did not come to burn people up. I came to rescue them" (Luke 9:54-56, author's paraphrase).

The poor disciples just could not get the hang of this mercy thing. After all, Jesus' behavior seemed contradictory. He would not let them burn up one Samaritan village, but he would kill a tree just because it had no fruit when he was hungry (see Matthew 21:19). Why did he act one way in one situation and the opposite in another? What was the difference?

Evidently there were some things that Jesus would not stand for. Just as evident, however, was the fact that he did not see himself as the Wrath of God. He did not walk the streets striking sinners blind and giving liars leprosy. If he had done that, he would have had a lot less trouble from the Pharisees.

The Pharisees were not suspicious of Jesus because of his miraculous works. They believed in the supernatural. Miracles, demons, angels and the resurrection all had a place in their theology. What they disliked about Jesus was that he worked miracles for those who *needed* them instead of those who deserved them. The Pharisees wanted justice, not mercy. They believed that bad people ought to have bad things in their lives. But all acts of mercy reverse what ought to be. If Jesus had turned the houses of the wealthy to gold and made the strong leap over buildings, he would not have run afoul of justice. It was not that he went about doing good that got him in trouble, it was that he did too much good to those who deserved evil. He healed sick people, forgave prostitutes and tax collectors and freed demoniacs. Mercy like that blots out justice. The Pharisees were worried about that kind of mercy getting loose in the streets. How would the good people know they were good and the bad people be reminded that they deserved to suffer?

UPSETTING THE APPLECART

The Pharisees were not comfortable with mercy. They wanted cause-and-effect justice. They believed that the lame had done something wrong that caused them to be lame. If the lame were made to leap for joy, they might think they had done nothing wrong, after all. They were just as good as the good people. Or worse, they might decide that the good people "needed" mercy just as they did. There is nothing quite so comforting to a smug, self-satisfied man with good eyes as the sight of a blind man tapping down the street.

We say to ourselves: *Look at him. I do not know why he is blind, but the fact is that he is, and I am not.* That is proof that things are as they should be. Sight is a privilege *only* as it compares with blindness. So when Jesus made blind people see, he upset the applecart of cosmic justice.

When Jesus heard that the Pharisees had cast out the blind man he had healed (see John 9), he found the man and asked him, "Do you believe in the Son of God?" Can you see the shocking implication of that question? The man was not even a believer, at least not a Christian in any New Testament sense. He had no faith in the name of Jesus. All he had was need—blind, dirty, stinking, unsaved need. Jesus did not heal him because he deserved it; he healed the blind man only because he needed it. His healing was a miracle of mercy. That is what Pharisees hate.

"Who is the Son of God?" the man asked Jesus. "Tell me so that I may believe in him."

"You're looking at him," Jesus answered. "Who do you think is talking to you right now?"

When the man fell down and worshiped him, Jesus said to the scowling Pharisees, "This is the judgment I brought into the world. Everyone is now divided into two groups. Those who need, and those who don't. Those who need sight will receive. Those who have no need will be made blind" (John 9:39, author's paraphrase).

The Pharisees howled, "What? Are we blind like this wretch here?"

"No," Jesus said. "You can see, and therefore you get no mercy. Your lack of need has cut you off from the mercy that only the needy and blind receive."

Jesus made the same statement about mercy in Matthew 9:10-13. He was again talking to the Pharisees, who were still griping and complaining, this time because he had called Matthew to be his disciple. When Matthew turned from being a tax collector to follow Christ, Jesus went in to eat with his friends who were, we understand from the Bible, a pretty sordid group. His presence among this gang of sinners excited the Pharisees.

"Why does Jesus eat with sinners?" they demanded.

Jesus' answer was maddeningly simple. "Only the sick need a physician. If you're well, you have no need of a doctor."

That settled it for the Pharisees. They were well. They did not need a doctor, nor did they need mercy.

In effect, Jesus was saying that such an attitude was one way to cut yourself off from God's mercy. This infuriated the religious Pharisees. They were not willing to admit to needing a doctor, but they also did not want God to meet the needs of those who confessed they needed one. The Pharisees declared: "Let the sick remain sick. Their disease tells their story. We are well. Let the Samaritans stand outside looking in. God should go outside to them? Hardly! That is their story. We are on the inside."

Of all the things that Jesus taught about God, his instruction on mercy got him in the most hot water. His troubles were always with the religious community. The barkeeps and prostitutes gave Jesus no problems. And the politicos were not much bothered with him until the religious insiders forced their hand.

GOD GIVES WHAT WE DON'T DESERVE

What did Jesus show about the nature of God that caused such a storm, and still does? Maybe the answer is found in the next thing Jesus said to the Pharisees when they protested the dinner at Matthew's house.

"Try to understand the meaning of this verse from Hosea," Jesus said, "'I will have mercy and not sacrifice'" (Matthew 9:13, author's paraphrase).

I know of a pastor who once tried to launch a Sunday morning ministry to families with HIV babies. A doctor and a nurse had agreed to keep the babies and supervise special care of them so their parents could go to church. This was to be done in another room apart from the regular nursery. This seemed like such a wonderful idea that the pastor was flabbergasted at the firestorm that erupted when he joyfully announced it to the church.

"If you announce this to the city," one man angrily told him, "you will have every HIV-positive person in town coming to this church."

"Yes," the pastor agreed with naive joy. "Isn't that great?"

It wasn't. At least not to that guy. And not to a lot of others.

"What if somebody with AIDS is sitting right on the same pew with me in church?" one woman demanded. "I could catch AIDS just by coming to church."

Scientific assurances to the contrary were cast aside as part of the conspiracy between the federal government and the homosexual agenda, and evidently, their pastor.

The angrier the parishioners got, the more confused the pastor got. "Look," he said. "We are not equivocating on sin. Homosexuality is a sin. But AIDS is not."

That statement was the straw that broke the camel's back for one man, who shouted, "I'm leaving this church. If you cannot see the connection between AIDS and sin, then I don't need to be under your teaching."

"I did not say there was no connection," the pastor replied. "Sometimes there is. The point I was making is that we can show mercy to the suffering, even if they are suffering for their sins."

"Romans, chapter one!" the parishioner yelled. "If God has decided to let them receive in their bodies the consequences for their sin, then we should not get in God's way. If we do, we will suffer. I do not intend to catch AIDS in church."

What was going on here? The underlying problem was differing views of the nature of God.

The man who left the church preached the same view of God as the Pharisees did. It was also the view of Job's friends—a view which proclaimed the sick should suffer. Somewhere, somehow, they had sinned, and now they were getting what they deserved.

This view differs greatly from that of the merciful, long-suffering father in Jesus' story of the Prodigal Son. In that parable God is tender, compassionate, quick to forgive and willing to embrace his returning son … with no strings attached. The father Jesus taught about did not give the boy what he deserved, but what he definitely did not deserve.

The real issue in such an unfortunate clash was also at

the crux of Jesus' constant conflict with the Pharisees. The darkness at the heart of a religious spirit always opts for a far narrower mercy than what Jesus showed. Each moment of ministry when Jesus, by his actions, revealed the wideness of God's mercy brought him into diametrical opposition to the spirit of the Pharisees. Mercy in action is where the fat always hits the fire.

SORDID PAST OR REPENTANT HEART?

One of Jesus' most tender acts of mercy happened at a dinner party. In Luke 7:36-50, the Master was eating at the house of a man called Simon the Pharisee. In the middle of the meal, a known prostitute rushed in and began to kiss Jesus' feet. Simon the Pharisee was horrified. *If this man were a real prophet*, he reasoned, *he would know this woman was a sinner.*

Of signal importance is the track of Simon's deductive reasoning. How did he know that Jesus had not discerned what a sinner she was? To Simon it was obvious:

A. no true man of God would let her kiss him.

B. Jesus was letting her do exactly that. Therefore,

C. Jesus must lack either discernment or holiness.

Either way, he couldn't be much of a prophet. Not if God is who Simon thought him to be—a sterile, merciless God, whose holiness is repulsed by the loving touch of unclean lips.

The most significant and revealing detail in the story is not anything Jesus did but what he did not do—he did not move. He sat right there, and with others watching, he let a notorious woman pour out physical affection on his exposed feet. I cringe at the thought of what might have been my own reaction. Would I have sat still for her tears and kisses? I rather imagine myself leaping away and shouting, "For God's sake, woman, stop that! These people will wonder where we met!"

But not Jesus. He did not draw away from her crimson past. He was more concerned about not wounding her further than about his or her reputation.

What does such a scene tell us about Jesus' idea of mercy? Much in every way. Here is a God more concerned with a repentant heart than a sordid past. Furthermore, he is able to discern the true heart of those who reach out to him. Simon, the Pharisee, entertained Jesus at a dinner party, but in his heart Simon condemned Jesus as a fraud. The woman, on the contrary, discerned the first man she had ever known who could be touched and not titillated, adored and not excited, loved and not lusted after. She found in him the first clean affection of her life, and Jesus was not willing to deprive her of it. What mercy!

WIDE MERCY OFFENDS

God's mercy is wide. His mercy did not stay in heaven's ivory halls but got down in the mud and the blood. The incarnate God wrestles with the thorny complications of humanity, never oversimplifying, never aghast at the perverse, sad, lonely horror of our flesh, yet always willing to show mercy to what we have made of ourselves.

For God, the watershed for mercy and justice is

religious pride. The Pharisees, the money changers and the religious leaders received severe lashings by both tongue and whip. They committed the two sins God evidently will not stand for: pride and condemnation. Their religious pride denied their own need for mercy. Their angry judgment denied mercy to everyone else.

The legalist looks at King David's adultery, murder, conspiracy, vengeful violence and life of polygamous sex and is baffled that David would still be a man after God's own heart. After David's sin with Bathsheba, the baby they conceived was evidently slain by the hand of the Lord. At this, the Pharisees among us purse their lips and applaud with stern dignity. The more "liberal" of our number howl in outrage that God could be so cruel. But when God blesses the marriage of David and Bathsheba, even to the point of putting their second child, Solomon, on the throne, the legalistic Pharisees shake their fists at a God who is "soft on immorality." The moral liberals shake their heads and begrudgingly allow God "that one," but why didn't he do that the first time?

The reasons perhaps lie close to God's sovereignty. He is a just God and he will not answer to us. Sin, like David's, unleashes tragic results. Divine mercy is not obligated to remove all those consequences. But in them, in the midst of them, there is mercy. The wideness in God's mercy manages to offend most everyone at one point or another. It is because of the Incarnation. If God had just stayed out of our world, waiting angrily for our least offense, or bored and withdrawn behind his mound of work, we could have dealt with him. But when he becomes flesh like our flesh, when he gets down in the muck and mire with us, we don't like it at all. "Either stay away," we shout at heaven, "or give us law. Either stay away and leave us to our devices or give us tables of stone."

The complication of divine mercy is its greatest proof of divinity. Sticky, complicated, messy mercy that is wider, far wider than we think, is the only way through the gate that is narrower than we like to pretend. Mercy is there for those who know their need of it. But such mercy will not be institutionalized or formalized. Mercy will not be laid against measuring tools and trimmed to fit our tiny frame of reference. And it will not be stretched to embrace our determination to go on in rebellion. Mercy, real mercy, is never simple, but it is always simply wonderful.

> There's a wideness in God's mercy,
> Like the wideness of the sea;
> There's a kindness in His justice,
> Which is more than liberty.
> There is welcome for the sinner,
> And more graces for the good;
> There is mercy with our Savior;
> There is healing in His blood.[1]

The Wash Rag

"Oh, Daddy!" she wailed, heaving again. "Oh, Daddy, I'm sorry."

"It's all right," he said, wiping the flecks of vomit from her mouth. "Go ahead. Get it all out."

She vomited one last time, but she was empty now. The dry heaving made her stomach ache like she had been hit with a bat. This was the sickest she had ever been, and she was so ashamed and confused that she could hardly think of anything to say beyond what she kept saying over and over again between the racking heaves.

"I'm sorry, Daddy. I'm just so sorry."

"I know," he kept whispering. "I know you are. We can beat this, baby. This is not going to ruin your life."

"I'm sorry, Dad. I did it again. I'm *so* sorry."

"I know," he whispered again as he lay her back against the pillows. "Go to sleep now. We'll figure out what to do tomorrow. It's going to be all right. I *promise* you. Sleep now, darling. Daddy's here."

She did sleep then. But not before she felt his big hands lay a cool, damp washcloth across her forehead. That cloth was wonderful. She did not open her eyes. She just let the thick wetness of the terry cloth lie cool and soft above her eyes. When she was a little girl and got sick he used to do that, put that cloth there, just like that, on her forehead. But she was not little anymore, and she was not exactly sick, but the washcloth still felt just as good. And her father was still there beside her, big and strong and forgiving. She put her hand on his and let the cool, wet rag soothe her. Ah, that washcloth. It felt so wonderful.

Four

The Mercy of Acceptance

Tennessee Williams' heartrending play *The Night of the Iguana* opens with a minister appealing to his congregation for help and understanding. He rips away his church mask and cries out for mercy, but his pathetic appeals terrify the people. They flee, literally running from him, until he is all alone. Shall Tennessee Williams, then, be numbered among the prophets?

For all its lip service to transparency, the American church fears it like the Black Death. We have settled for a pretended perfection that buys conditional acceptance. Like life imitating art imitating life, the church rejects real life with all its gritty humanity. We shun those who get very real.

OUR LONGING FOR BELONGING

We humans long to belong. Like the fear of falling, the terror of being ostracized is in us from the beginning. Just imagine five fifth-grade boys forming a club with their own secret handshake and codebook. At recess, let them meet in some secluded corner of the playground for their clandestine rendezvous, and watch the social contortions other boys are willing to endure just to be in the club.

Outsiders approach tentatively, pretending disinterest, hoping to ease the pain of their probable rejection. If the club were about acceptance, there would be no fear. But they know it's not. They know the club is about exclusivism, not about helping the fat or bespectacled or clumsy kids feel good about themselves. The club is not for them. It is for the inner circle, for reminding themselves that they are the chosen, select, elite who can see the others for the undesirables they really are.

The merciful answer of a merciful God rings sweet and pure from heaven for all the fat kids, and the nerdy ones, and the ugly ones and—wonderfully enough—even for the insiders in the club, if they will hear it. Our acceptance—full, final and perfect—is in Christ and him alone.

"Accepting Christ" is not the hope of humanity. Our blessed hope is that in Christ, God accepts us. "Blessed be the God and Father of our Lord Jesus Christ, who hath … made us accepted in the Beloved" (Ephesians 1:3, 6).

All my insecurities and fears about being found less than acceptable are swallowed up in him! Who dares to reject—who has the power to reject—one who has been accepted by the true and living God? To all the deserted children and abandoned wives and cuckolded husbands, to the outsiders and the weak, the acceptance of God is merciful indeed.

On the other hand, God's merciful acceptance is part of what makes Christianity such a hard sell among the upper crust. Jesus certainly discovered this. In Mark 12:37 we read, "The *common* people heard him gladly" (emphasis mine). Why? Painfully aware of their own commonness, they gladly welcomed a merciful and accepting

Savior who was willing to eat dinner with the riffraff. But it did nothing to endear Jesus to the Pharisees. The faith that welcomes lepers and outcasts holds faint allure for maharajahs and magnates. The message of acceptance beckons only the bedraggled, who know they need it. Elitism appeals, not to our need for mercy, but to that old sinful longing for the schoolyard "club."

The church must decide what it is about. Is it the merciful gathering of the lame and halt who need the acceptance of God? Or will it be the opera of the elite, where only the very best performers sing and dance for an audience that is worthy of them? That is a merciless picture, because in such a church I would live in cruel fear that my true condition might somehow be discovered. My spiritual energies would be expended not in struggling to be open and honest—God forbid!—but in a desperate fight to keep the mask in place.

KEEPING OUR MASK IN PLACE

By my junior year in high school, my prodigal tendencies had become legend in our small rural community, but by today's standards my high school sins were downright prosaic. I once rolled a pair of brass band cymbals down three flights of stairs during third period. The delicious noise was absolutely incredible! I felt immensely rewarded for my creativity, and the sentence of a month in detention hall seemed well worth the boost to my growing reputation.

In that same year I auditioned for and was awarded a

part in the class play. Not Broadway, to be sure, but still it was exciting to me. The part assigned to me was that of a priest ministering to a prisoner on death row. My big scene was a poignant one in which I, prayer book open, led the youthful convict toward the gallows, while reading Psalm 23. In rehearsals the scene was quite moving, and I fancied myself rather fetching in cassock and collar. I was especially excited about our opening, which we were to perform in an assembly for the entire school.

All went well until I stepped onto the stage dressed as a priest. At the sight of me, the student body erupted into gales of deafening, play-stopping laughter. The resulting furor is still known in local lore as the Big Riot of '65. As I stood sheepishly waiting for the noise to stop, my classmates rolled in the aisles, threw playbills in the air, and hurled sarcasm at the stage like rotten tomatoes until the principal finally had to restore order.

That is what we fear—that we will step out onto the stage of eternity in all our religious finery, and somebody will burst out laughing. The fear of being laughed at by "insiders" haunts most of us at some time or another. Some inner voice, in touch with our own fallenness, keeps insisting, "I don't belong on this stage. They're going to laugh!"

Our religious selves hope to get the costume right enough to fool the audience, whether that's heaven, hell, the church or the world. We rehearse our lines, pour on the makeup and keep fine-tuning our costume. With a touch here and a detail there, we keep striving for that desired authentic look. Why do we keep checking ourselves in the mirror? Because our costumes do little to allay our apprehensions that sooner or later some jerk in the back row will snicker, and the game will be up in one stupendously embarrassing moment.

Theater will never work if the audience sees nothing more impressive than the ludicrous sight of a classmate in an idiotic priest's suit. The singular contract between actor and audience that allows the play to go on is a mutually agreed upon suspended disbelief. The actors on the stage strut about and murder one another as if no one were watching. The audience must pretend that what they are seeing is real. To ruin a play, just turn to your neighbor and periodically explain, "Oh, that's not a real knife," or, "Don't worry, it's only ketchup."

Often we do the same in the church. We have a mutual agreement to suspend disbelief. I will ooh! and ahh! at your costume, but when I put mine on I expect some appreciation. Thus church becomes theater, and fellowship turns to façade.

Why all the playacting? That is the question that haunts us. We keep on covering up our insecurities and inadequacies with toupees and elevator shoes. Why? Because we are not sure we belong here. We worry: If it is a play, how did I get the part? Do my tights fit? Will anybody applaud?

The fear of exposure turns some into shallow pretenders. They may say their spiritual-sounding lines right on cue, but offstage they are empty. Without a clue as to who they really are, many spend their sad, false lives auditioning for whatever part is offered them.

This is true of the actors and actresses no matter what kind of play is being performed. It may be "high church" opera or the lowbrow, music-hall rowdiness of the Pentecostals. Some like the *Hall of the Mountain King.* Others prefer a good ol' Baptist version of the *Pirates of Penzance.* But if it's all just theater, what's the difference?

We cannot resolve this among ourselves. In the church we are both the actors and the audience. We just keep on joining and enlarging the neighborhood Church of the Codependent Bride until its very size commands the respect of the community. This is not, the architecture announces, some shabby little theater putting on second-rate versions of *The Music Man.* Look at it! This is Broadway! And I am a season ticket holder. I am part of that bright host that makes the church successful. And it, by its success, makes me know who I am. Defined by its obvious outward grandeur, it reaffirms me and my costume every time I drive up to the parking lot.

Please understand what I'm saying here. I am not criticizing the American mega-church, for churches of all sizes—large and small—lack mercy in their incessant demand for perfection. Not so sure? Just show up on Sunday morning in the wrong costume or say your lines with too much passion or kick too high in the chorus line. If everybody at church is playing the part of "Perfect Christian," I must put on my costume and say the lines or perish. There is no room for weaknesses and no tolerance for ugly warts popping up through the makeup.

The problem, however, is not just them but me. I cannot tolerate my own warts. Some Sunday, sooner or later, I put on my "Perfect Christian" costume and gaze unconvinced at my own image. It's not right. It doesn't fit. It doesn't work. They'll all know. I know!

When I am merely an actor on a stage, I have nothing to fall back on. When my costume drops around my ankles, there's no backstage voice whispering, "Hey, I see what you've done, but trust me, you belong here." If I hope to find confidence and a sense of belonging in what I do, in how I perform, I am doomed to the joyless insecurity of fear. I cannot succeed often enough. The payoff of the theater is today's applause. Its terrible, haunting fear is tomorrow's silence.

WHAT WE WANT
FROM THE CHURCH

Everything in life, especially childhood, cultivates all our latent insecurities. Surely the sense of being an unworthy, unwelcome outsider is among the most common and dark childhood memories. The playground cruelties pound remorselessly on little egos until they yield to the need to earn approval. Weight, size, shape, facial features, speech patterns or inabilities are pounced upon with relentless fury. Thoughtless and insensitive adults, unthinking teachers and sometimes even the best of parents can say some word or phrase that hammers the horrible truth home: Something is wrong with you! We learn early on, and perhaps no matter what we do, that we will not be acceptable.

That primary lesson learned, most of us spend our lives trying to find acceptance somewhere, somehow, by someone. The longing to belong drives some into boardrooms and others into barrooms. Some of the most "successful" people in the world are consumed with the same terrible self-doubt that eats at many of the worst failures. Indeed, most adults—unfortunately no less in the church than in the world—come to realize that their lifelong battle for acceptance has been futile. Having pumped all that iron, earned all that money and done all that their friends demanded, they face the terrible secret. It didn't work.

The system is merciless. First it convinces us that we are unacceptable, then it announces a price of admission that is phenomenally inflated and wrapped in an interest rate so high that instead of ever paying our way in, we just get deeper in debt. Growing in our inner conviction that we don't really belong, we pay through the nose for acceptance that never fully comes and, even if it does, won't last. At the end of it we are what we thought we were to start with: bankrupt outsiders who never really learned all the secret lingo of the inner circle.

All too often we want the church to do the wrong thing for us. When we turn our lonely, baleful eyes on each other and plead for affirmation and reinforcement in a religious community, belonging to one another takes precedence over belonging to God. The guys at Temple Beth Pharisee handed out look-alike robes and tassels, and all learned the same prayers, even devoted themselves to the secret rule book. The problem was that Rule One was to love God more than the rules, more than the tassels and even more than being seated with the other elders who obeyed the rules.

THE ANTIDOTE FOR THE POISON OF PERFORMANCE

Jesus preached that it was possible to find acceptance with God and never be in good standing with the Elders Club. He reduced the rule book to Rule One and informed half-castes, outcasts, Samaritans and sinners that their heavenly God wanted to be their heavenly Father. That is what got him killed. Mercy, it appears, is also pretty thin among Pharisees.

Jesus was not crucified because he raised the dead and healed the sick. He was not slain because he claimed to be the Son of God, though that was closer to the issue. What got Jesus killed was being the Son of God, proving it with power and then inviting others into the family without requiring them to join the Club first.

"Other sheep I have, that are not of this fold," he said in John 10:16, 17. "Them also I must bring, and they shall hear my voice; and there shall be one fold, and one shepherd. Therefore doth my Father love me, because I lay down my life."

In more modern language, those verses might read something like this. "You guys think you have the only club. But I want a family, not a club. I AM the club. I AM the president. My Father loves me, and I want all the people looking for meaning in all the clubs to join me, so that my Father may be their Father. I AM willing to die for them to join."

All members in good standing were furious, but the disenfranchised, the hookers and bartenders knew mercy when they heard it. They still do. But what is wonderful news to the outsiders sounds pretty unsettling to the club officers.

The message of the gospel, in modern evangelical circles, has become limited to the good news of forgiveness and heaven. Well, isn't that enough? It is wonderful, and if it were all God offered, it would still be an amazing graciousness. But it isn't all God offers. What God offers is the mercy of adoption, full membership into his family, not his fan club. The good news is not just a God who forgives but a Father who receives.

When the Prodigal Son returned from the pigsty, he told his father, "I hate the pig club now. It did *not* work for me. Now that I really see how good you are, I want to join your fan club. I just want to sleep and eat and work with the other members."

"Are you crazy?" said his father, laughing and weeping at the same time. "You're my son! My child!"

"But I'm dirty."

"You're not dirty!" the father shouted, as he gleefully put his arm around the boy and they started back up to the house. "You're my son."

The fatherhood of God is the antidote for the poison of performance. His perfect love casts out all my fear of failure. The dread of disappointing him is swallowed up, not in my resolve to do better next year, but in a relationship so secure that it cannot be broken when I forget my lines.

The Birthmark

The old man watched them as though his life depended on it. In a way his life did depend on the outcome of the madonna-and-child scene being played out before him. They had no idea he was watching. Probably they wouldn't have minded anyway. Certainly the baby wouldn't mind. He was one of those boy babies who looked like a boy even in infancy. He was fat and jolly, and he kicked his tiny bare feet in the air as if he hadn't a care in the world.

There was no way that at eight or nine months the little fellow could know what he looked like with that bright red splotch running across his face. This mark was not the kind of soft temporary port wine mark that faded in a few months. It was thickened, raised. *Someday*, the old man thought to himself, *that little fellow will look in a mirror and hate the sight of himself.*

But it was not the baby the old man wanted to watch. It was the mother. She was a gorgeous pixie with wheat for hair and eyes like the Mediterranean in May. If she had lost her figure during pregnancy, she had certainly regained it quickly and wonderfully. She was a tiny thing with the waist of a wasp and enough curves to turn any man's head.

He had to know, had to find out. How could he get her attention? He was not going to leave the waiting room until his question was answered. He could just ask her, he supposed. No, that would never do. She was young and would be offended by such a question, should be offended. But he had to know.

Look at them. Look at her laughing and nuzzling the little fellow as though he were the most beautiful baby that ever lived. The old man wheeled his chair closer. They didn't mind. People in hospital waiting rooms seem to assume some temporary intimacy with each other. No one sits in such a place unless they share some human woe. They have something in common and it makes them all close and more unguarded than usual.

"He loves to laugh," the young beauty said, turning to look him in the eye.

"I see that," he replied. "I see that he does. Are you here for him to see the doctor?"

"Him?" The girl laughed, and her smile was so lovely that he knew she could reach any male of any age anywhere with but half its power. "Lord, no! He's as healthy as a horse. My husband's mother is having surgery tomorrow. He's inside with her. But this big guy is too rowdy for a hospital room. What about you? Why are you here?"

"What do you think?" The words came out more bitterly than he had meant them to.

"What?" she asked innocently. "The legs?"

"Of course," he snapped. *Easy now*, he scolded

himself, *don't run her off. Get the answer. Get the answer!* "Lost 'em both. Truck wreck. Funny. Sometimes I think I can still feel my feet."

"I've heard that," she said.

"You have?"

"Yes. Or read it maybe. When do you get to go home?"

"I don't know." He rolled the wheelchair closer until the bandaged stubs of his legs were nearly touching the edge of the sofa. "My grandson is coming to see me today. It's the first time since the wreck. Your boy is real solid. How old is he?"

"Eight months," she answered.

"I was gonna guess eleven months."

"His father is a football coach."

"Ah," he said. "And you were a cheerleader."

She smiled. "Majorette."

"You're beautiful ... like a movie star."

She laid her tiny hand on his arm. "What a nice thing to say. You could teach the young guys a thing or two about giving compliments."

"I'm seventy-eight."

"I'd never have guessed," she lied. He looked eighty-five, and he knew it. This was a really nice girl.

"I'm afraid I'll scare my grandson," he admitted. "You know, with these ..."

"No," she said, gathering her fat giggling infant into her arms. "To him you'll just be Grandpa."

"Is that true? How do you know?"

"I know. Look, I have to go change Mikey here. Don't worry about your grandson. Other people may see a man without legs. He'll only see his grandfather. That's the way it works. Don't worry."

With that she and the baby were gone, laughing and cooing at one another. The old man never got to ask. All he had wanted to know was if a young woman so beautiful was ever embarrassed by a baby so horribly disfigured. She didn't seem to be, but he still wished he had asked her anyway.

He turned the wheelchair to face the door. They would be here any minute. He pulled the blanket across the bandages. No use to let his grandson see that first thing. Then he jerked the blanket away. Let him see the truth!

At last he replaced the blanket and recombed his hair. Any minute now. He smiled at the empty door and held out his arms, practicing for the thousandth time. He thought he could hear a child's footsteps down the hall. They quickened. Now he could hear his daughter cautioning his grandson not to run.

"Grandpa!" the boy shouted, hustling across the tile floor and into his lap. "Wow! Cool. Take me for a ride. How fast can you go? These don't hurt, do they? We had ice cream downstairs. Go, Grandpa! Go fast!"

Five

The Mercy of Restoration

I have one rod and reel among my small collection that is special to me. Today I love it, but I didn't when I first saw it. I was fishing and thought a small limb had snagged my hook. I finally pulled the "limb" free of the muck on the bottom of the lake and reeled in the nastiest rod and reel I had ever seen. I wondered if some frustrated fisherman had pitched it overboard. Whether by accident or by passionate intent, the thing had been lost to the deep. Upon dredging it up, I claimed the ancient right of salvage.

I scraped off enough mud to see that it had once been an expensive rod and a fine spinning reel. But they were in pitiful shape. The mire had corroded the surface and penetrated the gears. I spent days cleaning and repairing the rod and reel. I used an entire can of WD-40 and a new spool of line, but it was worth it. When I was done, I had a good, useable rod and reel.

But it is not as good as new. The time spent lying in the mud left an indelible mark. On the other hand, had it never been lost in the mud, the rod and reel would never have been mine. Even now some dirt works its way out of the gears from time to time, and the reel is sometimes a bit cranky. But I glory in that faded rod and reworked reel. I guess it reminds me of … well … me.

IS RESTORATION A FAIRY TALE?

Our darkest fear is that we can never be right again. Most Christians believe God has forgiven them their sins. But for many, restoration seems like a fairy tale. We have trouble believing that God will restore what we have lost because of our sin. How could he be so merciful? We have taken to heart Thomas Wolfe's words that we can't go home again. And in many ways he was right. It's not possible to go back into the old neighborhood and play "Kick the Can" with the same innocent, carefree minds, or to sleep on our mother's lap, dreaming the dreams of unsullied children. All the king's angels can never put Humpty Dumpty together again.

But is that what restoration means? Will restoration come if we "go back home" and find our shadows, think happy thoughts and fly away to never-never land? I don't think so.

Restoration is not God making men into boys, it is God making men into sons, and women into daughters. In that sublime sense, Wolfe was horribly wrong. We may not ever squeeze back into our lost yesterdays, but we can reenter a wonderful garden once closed to us and sealed with the imperial seal.

Marriages and minds and bodies can be restored. Consciences once seared by sin can be restored. Jobs and fortunes squandered by sin and extravagance can be restored. God is a God of great mercy, and his mercy sets the prisoner free—and not just from inner bondage. God can take convicts out of prisons and give them lives of dignity and productive fulfillment. Ask Charles Colson.

Does it mean that every person who gets saved is guaranteed that every aspect of his or her life will be restored? Will all broken marriages be healed? Will all convicts become heads of prison ministries? Obviously not. But in all lives whose potential has been squandered by sin, God is willing to work in restoration mercy.

Not everything will be made as good as new. Some people, like Jacob, will always walk with a limp. Some fallen ministers will serve God as truck drivers and never be let back into the pulpit. But even in those lives, God will restore much in other ways. In still others, God will give it all back. He is the God who can put poor Humpty Dumpty back together again.

PARADISE REGAINED

When Adam and Eve were exiled from Eden, God placed cherubim and a flaming sword at the entrance. The sword turned every way, vigilantly guarding against human re-entry, whether it came from the east or the west, or by works, or by religion or by any other means. In the Fall, humankind lost more than innocence. In the garden Adam had walked and talked with God in the cool of the evening. In Eden, Adam had meaningful work as God's steward gardener and intimacy as his friend and son. Because of his sin, Adam inherited not only a world full of violence and death but a heart filled with insecurity, loss of meaning and alienation. Before the Fall, Adam had not been, as some think, a naked, work-free Pan, lolling about on the island of the lotus eaters. In Eden he had known his origin, his purpose and his meaning.

A mercy that is narrower than that promised by Jesus could simply forgive us our trespasses and promise us heaven when we die—without restoring us to relationship and purposeful living in the here and now. But the second Adam restores what the first Adam squandered. The church and the world need to be reminded that God's mercy means more than forgiveness. We are not merely forgiven and left outside to press our dirty little noses against the windows of Eden. We are received, adopted and given a share in the Father's business, not as bunkhouse hired hands but as sons and daughters with an inheritance undefiled even by us.

"I'M GOING TO MAKE YOU A PARTNER IN MY FIRM..."

An excellent example of God's desire to restore is seen in the meeting between Peter and Jesus in Luke 5. Simon was overcome by his own sin and the Master's holiness. Having seen Jesus' power to fill his empty fishing nets when no one else was catching any fish, Peter knew that Jesus was more than just some guy with a serious knack for fishing. Something in the moment, something in the Lord's eyes, knocked Peter to his knees in wounded, sincere introspection. The piercing eyes of God devastated Peter. In the presence and power of Jesus, Peter's sin-consciousness made him feel his alienation from God. This was not about Adam's sin. There, in that moment, it was painfully, excruciatingly about Simon Peter's sins. "I have departed from you," he confessed (see Luke 5:8, author's paraphrase). "Now it's only right that you should depart from me. I don't deserve to be in your presence."

"Don't be afraid of what you've just seen," Jesus said with a smile as warm and comforting as the sun upon the lake. "You've just seen the power of anointed fruitfulness. And I'm going to make you a partner in my firm just as Zebedee over there did for his sons, James and John. From now on you will fish for men."

At these words Peter immediately left everything: his livelihood, his lifestyle and his natural skills. Why? Because he was enthralled by the mercy of restoration. That he, in the light of what he knew himself to be, should be restored to the position which Adam had lost was enough to woo Peter away from his business. The issue was not legalism as some seem to mean by phrases such as "God has a claim on your life." It was joyful! Peter did not just obey a command to catch men. He leapt at the merciful offer of being restored to participation in the main business of God.

We have too often lost sight of the great, grand mercy revealed in God's invitation to labor in his vineyard and fish his stormy seas, then chat with him on the beach when evening comes. We do not deserve this, and it is not a burden. It is a privilege afforded us wayward rebels by a mercy so wide and a generosity so munificent that we can scarce believe it.

I have a dear friend named Jim, who is a talented and capable preacher, but he was once a fearsome man of the streets. Even though Jim was into drugs and alcohol and serious crime, God never gave up on him. Wounded and arrested in the attempted armed robbery of a drugstore, Jim still carries a scar and the weight of a criminal record. At one point he was a desperate, heroin-addicted creature, sleeping in dumpsters, and at another time he even pimped for a living. Can God forgive such a man? Certainly! We would not even get an argument on that. Remember the thief on the cross, some would cry. But the thief on the cross died soon after. He went from the place of forgiveness straight into paradise. On the same day! The thief didn't have to go back to church.

Jim, like the rest of us, had to go on living after finding God's forgiveness. Salvation doesn't blot out the consequences of a sordid past. He was still a lonely ex-con living in the Chicago Teen Challenge center. He was long on a police record and short on education, training and opportunities. What if he were forgiven? Heaven was a long way off. What did the restoration mercies of God mean for him, a burned-out felon?

Years later I stood side by side with this ex-criminal on the platform of one of America's largest churches. Distinguished, graying elegantly at the temples and impeccably dressed, Jim winked broadly at his wife, a former Salvation Army officer, and their three children. I heard him singing the praises of God in a fine, clear tenor, and then he preached the Word of Grace with power. I knew that I was seeing the mercy of restoration before my very eyes.

Any child knows this didn't happen in a day. It took Jim years of living in a Teen Challenge facility; years of driving a truck and signing up for correspondence courses; years of taking every ministry opportunity that presented itself. Years of waiting and working and being faithful. Years. But still God's restoration power had brought it all to pass.

RESTORATION REVEALS LORDSHIP

God's merciful restoration is clearly demonstrated in the Old Testament and in the New. Manasseh, who ruled Judah for fifty-five years, led the nation by precept and example into new levels of depravity (see 2 Chronicles 33:1-9). In fact *Manasseh* became symbolic of debauchery and idolatry. He worshiped the stars, built pagan altars, practiced human sacrifice with his own children and baptized himself in witchcraft. Manasseh even erected a pagan idol in the Temple of Solomon (see 2 Chronicles 33:7).

God sent prophets to rebuke him, but Manasseh rejected them. One prophet even warned that God would wipe out Jerusalem as one wipes a dish and turns it upside down on the drain rack (see 2 Chronicles 33:10; 2 Kings 21:13). But the king would not listen. We are told that for an answer he filled Jerusalem's streets with a river of innocent blood. Presumably, the blood of prophets was in that gruesome stream.

Finally God allowed Manasseh to be punished. The Assyrians ravished Jerusalem with unutterable cruelty. The temple was sacked, the city was looted and burned, the population was enslaved and King Manasseh was taken in chains to a dungeon in Babylon.

When life and history are merciless, men often seek

the mercy of God. That's what Manasseh did. In deep contrition he acknowledged his sins and their dreadful consequences. "And when he was in affliction, he besought the Lord, his God, and humbled himself greatly before the God of his fathers, and prayed unto him" (2 Chronicles 33:12, 13). Humility and remorse transformed his prison cell into a confessional.

Jailhouse religion? What other kind is there? Something, some outward circumstance or inner turmoil, some fear or shame, drives us into our Father's arms in search of the mercy we do not deserve. No one cries out for mercy until they know they need it. Whatever "prison" reveals that to us becomes a place of sacramental mercy and the door through which we pass from destruction, not just to forgiveness, but to restoration.

A little-known verse in 2 Chronicles 33:13 holds all the world of mercy in its simple words. "And [Manasseh] prayed unto [God]; and [God] was entreated by him, and heard his supplication, and brought him again to Jerusalem into his kingdom. *Then Manasseh knew that the LORD, He was God*" (emphasis mine).

God's power to restore is not the question. It is no less a demonstration of God's power to put a king in prison than it is to make a prisoner a king. Manasseh broke before God's justice. But God's restoration convinced him that the Lord is God. What Manasseh had lost—his nation, his liberty, his honor and his throne—God restored. Manasseh's personal walk with God was restored as well. "And [Manasseh] repaired the altar of the LORD, and sacrificed on it" (2 Chronicles 33:16).

CAN A FAILED MINISTRY
BE RESTORED?

The end of Acts 12 introduces the story of an intriguing young man named John Mark. He joined the apostle Paul in Jerusalem and journeyed with Paul and Barnabas, first to Antioch and then on a missionary journey that included Seleucia, Cypress, Paphos and Perga in Pamphylia.

Perhaps the trip was an overly ambitious one for a first missions experience. Or maybe John Mark was too easily discouraged, or just plain homesick. Whatever the reason, he abandoned the team in Perga and went home to Jerusalem.

No reason could have justified such an early departure to the choleric apostle Paul. Long on determination and short on patience, Paul determined never to use John Mark again. To Paul it was a useless risk to depend on a proven failure when the stakes were as high as the missionary expansion of the kingdom of God. I can almost hear Paul say, "No! We'll not take John Mark. The best indicator of future behavior is past behavior." To Paul's way of thinking, and I must say that I am fully sympathetic, John Mark was a loser. Why pour good money after bad?

Barnabas saw it otherwise. The boy could be, must be restored. Barnabas, whose name means "son of consolation," saw John Mark as too good a minister to be wasted. He was determined to see John Mark restored, not just to missions and ministry, but to the confidence of church leadership as well.

This contention caused so sharp a division between

Paul and Barnabas that on the next mission journey they went in different directions. Paul took Silas and went back to Syria. Barnabas, with young John Mark under his wing, sailed to Cyprus.

I see several lessons in this. First, Paul was a great man of God, but he was not the man that a wounded and discouraged John Mark needed. Barnabas, the "son of consolation," was the perfect candidate to patiently tutor John Mark back to trustworthy ministry. It is testimony not only to the tender discipleship of Barnabas but to God's mercy of restoration that John Mark was saved, not just for the kingdom but for meaningful ministry.

Second, we see that restoration has a process. (Look for more about this in the next chapter.) Barnabas was not just declaring John Mark fully fit. He was, however, refusing to declare him forever unfit. Time, teaching, accountability and right relationships are all part of the process of restoration. So is humble obedience on the part of the one being restored. The youthful John Mark submitted to Barnabas' authority for as long as it took.

Third, if all criteria are met, sooner or later amnesty must be granted. Paul was not the man to spend the time restoring a kid like John Mark, but neither was he an unforgiving tyrant. It is a testimony to all of them— Barnabas' patient love, John Mark's humble submission and Paul's practical good grace—that restoration found its final stamp of approval in a single, simple endorsement. "Take Mark," Paul wrote years later, "and bring him with thee; for he is profitable to me for the ministry" (2 Timothy 4:11).

Nearly twenty years ago, I heard that a young minister

friend had resigned from his church. I found the boy high on drugs and angry at the world. He reluctantly agreed to go with me to a crusade I was preaching, but once there, he began the long, painful journey back.

He was faithful and patient. God was faithful and full of mercy. It was the recipe of restoration, and now that young man is the distinguished pastor of a sizable church.

Recently another man reminded me of that pastor's dreary collapse all those years ago. "What do you think?" he asked me. "Do you think he's really out of all that for good?"

"What I think," I told the man, "is that the God who restored John Mark is the same yesterday, today and forever."

To doubt the possibility of restoration is to doubt the character and power of God. Some may not be restored. Some may try and fail. Some may abort the process. But for the humble and penitent, there is mercy not just to forgive but to restore.

The Village

Kafonga was not a large village, but its fifty or so thatched roofs nestled between the Bandu Ridge and the river made a lovely sight. The inhabitants of Kafonga knew that if they ever quit hacking at its creeping tentacles, the forest would devour the village in only a few years, not even to remember that people had ever lived there.

But they neither hated nor feared the jungle. They were forest people. This dense woodland was all they knew or cared to know of the world. It was not their adversary, nor was it their domain. They did not think of themselves as the owners of the forest. It housed them. It let them stay and plant some yams and make their fufu, and it did not resent their hunting and foraging. But its relentless power reminded them that they were temporary guests. They knew the high bluff of the Bandu Ridge looking down so sternly on their rooftops provided protection, not restriction. They did not go beyond it, because there was nothing they wanted or needed. The escarpment could be climbed. Many had done it. But on the other side was another world full of strange people without decency.

Some of these strange ones had trekked over the rocky backbone of the Bandu Ridge and visited Kafonga. That these visitors were of a different color and wore strange garments was not shocking to the people of Kafonga. Did not birds have different plumage? Still, they were all birds. The habits and tools of these visitors from beyond the Bandu were interesting, but everyone agreed they were useless in Kafonga.

The problem with these visitors was that they were rude, selfish and unhappy people. They wanted to hoard things and hide things. This is no good in a small village. Worst of all, they were filled with lust and violence. Around these outsiders no woman was safe, and any man who crossed them was in grave danger. Having observed all this, the people of Kafonga determined never to cross the Bandu Ridge.

But some young people would not listen to this. Occasionally one would leave, usually in the night, never to return again. The village would grieve with the family because they knew that no one from Kafonga would come to a good end among such a greedy, selfish and lustful people. No one knew what became of those who left. They just never returned.

That is, they never returned until Etuba came back. When the villagers saw him, they knew that all their worst fears for the others were confirmed. He was sick and weak and blind in one eye. But his family danced with joy, and the village elders called for a feast. Everyone was excited. Etuba was alive again. At last someone had returned from beyond the Bandu Ridge.

They nursed Etuba tenderly. His mother pounded fufu for him to eat, his father caught fish in the river and his sisters searched for special fruit from the jungle. Etuba received all this attention with gratitude and humility. He was glad to be home. The people beyond the Bandu had used him cruelly and corrupted him more than he realized. He was changed, and he wondered if he would ever again fit into life at Kafonga.

He could not hunt, because his blind eye had

spoiled his aim. When his shots went wide, the other men pretended not to notice, but Etuba could see the grief and embarrassment in their eyes. He got over the sickness he had come home with, but his body was weakened, and though he gradually got stronger, Etuba doubted he would ever be the same. All this, of course, made him unappealing to the village girls, so Etuba was lonely.

At times he even considered going back over the Bandu Ridge, but this thought seemed crazy to him. What would happen to him this time? He might lose the other eye. A sickly, one-eyed man might scale the ridge and find Kafonga, but a blind man could never return. No matter if he never married or never became an excellent hunter again, he was better off—far better off—in Kafonga.

There was one thing that Etuba could do really well. Like his father, Etuba was a patient and sensitive fisherman. He seemed to have an ability to know where the big fish were and could hook them when no one else could.

After some time, other men in the village began to ask Etuba to teach them to fish, which he was happy to do. They gave him gifts, and in this way he prospered, which gained him respect. When several years passed, Etuba married. At last he was becoming a full-fledged and fully accepted participant in village life. He was happy again in Kafonga.

Then came the night of the big council meeting.

All the men of the village sat in the chief's house considering the terrible question of whether to move the village. The game in the jungle was growing scarce, and some men thought they should abandon Kafonga and move higher up toward the Bandu Ridge.

Etuba knew this was a mistake, but in humility he kept silent. Who was he to speak? Why should anyone listen to him? But in his heart he knew they were wrong. The game was just as scarce up on the steeper slopes of the Bandu, and up there they would be further from the river. They would also be more exposed to the world beyond the Bandu. Etuba knew the answer was to stay where they were and become better fishermen.

At last he could contain himself no longer. He stood and said all these things to the council of men. Most could see the wisdom in the words, but they were uncomfortable that it was Etuba who had spoken them. Others, who were jealous of his fishing skills, mocked him and sneered. Who was he to speak? they demanded. He who had failed the village and been foolish enough to leave Kafonga had nothing to teach them. The land beyond the Bandu, they shouted, had made him a fool, and he should be silent.

Finally, the oldest man in the council stood to speak. Everyone was silent and respectful. They were amazed at his words. "Perhaps," he said, "it was not

Etuba who failed the village. Perhaps the village had failed Etuba. We were not able to teach him enough wisdom to stay here, but the pain and loss he endured taught him enough wisdom to return. Let's listen to him," said the ancient council member. "Any man who has lost an eye beyond the Bandu may know what foolishness really is. Any man who has come home may be wiser than all of us."

That was the end of it. They received Etuba's wisdom and stayed at Kafonga. After that Etuba knew that he also belonged to Kafonga. He was still blind, of course. But the fish found no advantage in this.

Six

Mercy in Process

I remember when my younger brother came home from his first day of school.

"Well," my mother said to the new first-grader. "What did you think of school?"

"It was OK, I guess," he replied with a shrug. "But not something I'd want to do every day."

None of us wanted the job of telling him that school was, in fact, something he was going to do and do and do, all day, every day, day after day, for many years. My brother was thinking of school like the Calvinist who fell down the stairs and said, "Thank God that's over!" It was, sadly for him, only beginning.

Modern Christians tend to be so event-oriented that the method of mercy appears quaint at best and tedious at worst. We love to sing "I once was blind but now I see." We are not so enthused about singing "I once was blind but now I see a little better."

THE RETURN OF FIVE BLESSINGS

When the repentant turns to God in genuine humility and true contrition, the mercy of restoration begins its work. From prison, divorce, scandal and an assortment of other pits we dig ourselves into, God can beautifully restore us.

Restoration is a fivefold mercy—the return of five blessings to a life. This pentagon of graces is clearly blueprinted in Revelation 22. The passage is a reference to the final restoration where, in a new heaven, the river of life will flow undiluted. Obviously, nothing in life now will be as perfect as then, but the text is rich with insight into how restoration works. In seeing how God will restore, we come to understand how he does restore.

> And he showed me a pure river of water of life, clear as crystal, proceeding out of the throne of God and of the Lamb. In the midst of the street of it, and on either side of the river, was there the tree of life, which bore twelve kinds of fruits, and yielded her fruit every month; and the leaves of the tree were for the healing of the nations. And there shall be no more curse, but the throne of God and of the Lamb shall be in it, and his servants shall serve him; And they shall see his face; and his name shall be in their foreheads. And there shall be no night there; and they need no lamp, neither light of the sun; for the Lord God giveth them light, and they shall reign for ever and ever.
>
> REVELATION 22:1-5

Imagine that on each side of this life-giving river there is a door, and over each doorway is the name of one of the five mercies. Inside is a continuous passageway that leads around the whole, so that no matter where one enters, whether at number one or number three, all will eventually be made whole. The process of restoration is the mercy of God for all the disinherited castaways of this world who have lain so long in the mud they can hardly find hope to believe. The five faces of restoration mercy are:

- Purpose in life
- The knowledge of God
- Identification with God
- Light from God
- Dominion with God

Purpose in Life

"His servants shall serve him" (Revelation 22:3).

God only knows the billions of dollars and countless kilowatts of emotional and psychological energy that have been wasted by people in search of purpose. Many plunge through relationships, jobs and avocations in a frantic madness that is both terrifying and tragic to watch.

A weekend farmer who once lived near us let his new BMW roll backward into his lake. How this happened we were never quite sure, but he swore he had backed up into the lake to get his fishing gear out of the trunk. When he got out to go around to the trunk, he accidentally left the car in reverse. At least that was his story.

What we do know is that he then backed up his new tractor to the lake in order to tow out the submerged BMW. When he got down to attach the tow chain, the tractor rolled back onto the BMW, smashing the front in and driving it even further into the muddy lake bottom.

Unwilling to admit defeat, he then ran a line underneath the tractor from a winch on the rear to the cross-beam on the barn. But the weight of the tractor, now hopelessly enmeshed in the bumper and grill of the nearly destroyed luxury car, was greater than he realized. He watched with horror as the winch inexorably cranked the line in under the tractor, pulling the barn roof into the lake on top of the two stranded vehicles.

Many Americans do the same thing every day. In their search for meaning, they pour vehicles, possessions, wives, husbands, hobbies and addictions into the bottomless lake of their own unfulfilled lives. The insatiable demand for more, whatever that means at the moment, will finally pull the roof down. Nothing will fill a life that, like a black hole, sucks up money, pleasure and other people. I think of all the articles in various magazines that promise an explained life to any woman bold enough to break free of the traditional trap of husband and children. Domesticity is the great male lie, they say. Then I meet a hard-eyed business-woman on an airplane who tells me that at fifty-four she is twice divorced, childless in both marriages, chronically depressed and worried that she is addicted to sleeping pills. "Getting it all" can mean winding up with nothing.

And then there are the male-oriented articles that fuel the engine of drivenness, pushing male executives up the steel rails of success. Just as empty, equally addicted and riddled with guilt, they seduce their secretaries, trade luxury cars and buy real estate in a desperate effort to silence the frightening voice that keeps whispering, "This is not working. This is *not* working!"

True meaning in life comes from being owned by God. For the servant of God, ownership provides definition and explanation of purpose: servants serve their master. How incredibly simple! We are not what we own or earn or learn or even feel. We are his forever. And to be allowed to serve God is an act of divine mercy. God does not have to let me serve. I am, at my best, unprofitable, unworthy and ineffective. God has a voice. People have heard it. He does not *need* mine. Many of us learned in Sunday school that God has no hands but our hands, but it isn't true. He can say, do or make *anything* he wants without my help. In allowing me to serve, he is not being merciful to the world. *He is being merciful to me.*

I have a friend who once prowled the elite corridors of power as a top executive in a large corporation. He was saved as an adult, and his values were transformed. Now in retirement he tutors math to poor black children at an inner-city elementary school. I asked why, and he said, "It's simple. I need to serve. I have a paid-for lake house and a luxury car and more money than I can spend. But when I kneel down by a student's desk and help her learn to do long division, I come alive. It's the greatest work experience I've ever had."

"The real question," he added, "is not why I tutor. That seems obvious to me. The question to me is, why would God let me? I've been a pretty tough hombre. Why would God give me moments of such tenderness and fulfillment with these children? Why would he do that?"

Mercy—God's wide mercy—restores us with purpose.

The Knowledge of God

"They shall see his face" (Revelation 22:4).

A prosecuting attorney was trying to convict an executive charged with embezzlement. In order to impeach the man's character, he called the man's secretary to the stand.

"Tell me," demanded the district attorney, "were you and the defendant intimate?"

"No," she responded forlornly. "Mostly we just had sex."

We may not know what intimacy is or how to find it, but we know when we don't have it. In today's plastic and steel world, precious few have *any* sense of intimacy, let alone intimacy with God.

Alienation is inevitably the cold, hard fruit of an advanced technocracy. Our TV screens entertain us, but they do not relate to us. In fact, when the TV is the center of attention, all present face it, not each other. Alienation is heightened by such a corporate focus on the inanimate other. Sharing the same visual experience is not intimacy. Sharing ourselves is intimacy.

After Adam's fall into sin, God asked, "Adam, where are you?"

He had never asked that before. Indeed, he did not have to ask it that time. God knew exactly which bush Adam cowered behind, now suddenly and painfully aware of his nakedness. God's question underscored the separation that had taken place. The two friends who had walked and talked together in the cool of the evening now cried out to each other across the universe.

"Adam, where are you?" God asked.

"Where are you?" Adam shouted back. "I used to see your face. Now I can barely even hear your voice."

"What have you done?" God asked. "Tell me quick. The hiddenness of your sin is widening the gap between us."

"You're breaking up," Adam wailed. "I'm losing you!"

But God in his mercy invites you and me back into his presence. Indeed, his promise of reentry is crucial to Revelation 22's glorious statement of paradise restored. "Blessed are they that do his commandments, that they may have right to the tree of life, and may ENTER IN THROUGH THE GATES into the city" (Revelation 22:14, caps mine).

For a time Adam slammed the door shut on intimacy with God, but God's mercy in Jesus Christ reopened it forever.

Left outside are those who insist upon practicing magic arts, and the sexually immoral, as well as murderers, idolaters and liars (see Revelation 22:15). God will not restore those who don't want to be restored. Heaven will not be full of murderers and liars. But it will be full of those who once were. For now the repentant find in the secret place of prayer and worship the tender fatherly embrace we once fled. We can snuggle close and gaze once more into the face of our Father. In Christ, our sins are forgiven, our intimacy restored.

Years ago in the little village of Boca de Juan Capitán in north Mexico, I met an amazing teenage girl. Having been the sexual plaything of most of the boys in the squalid collection of thatched huts, she finally found Christ one night in a tiny village church. Her changed lifestyle proved an inconvenience to the local thugs, who ambushed her on the way to church one night and brutally gang-raped her.

Rather than degrading her, however, it nearly made her a contemplative saint. Constant prayer, forgiveness and the restoring mercy of God put an intimidating radiance to her countenance. No one hurt her again. When I met her I was moved, not only by the story but by the wrenching depth in her eyes.

"How did you do it?" I asked. "How did you find such total victory in this terrible thing?"

"*En este mundo no hay misericordia. Pero en la cara de Dios, oh, hermano Marcos, en su cara ...*" She didn't finish. It was as if she couldn't find the words to describe what she had seen. Through the years I've remembered what that girl said. In English it would mean something like this: "In this world there is no mercy. But in the face of God—oh, Brother Mark, in his face ..." Shattered by a nightmare experience among sordid brutes, humanity at its most depraved fallenness, she was restored by nothing less than the mercy of God. The knowledge of God restored what the knowledge of evil might have destroyed.

Identification with God

"And his name shall be in their foreheads" (Revelation 22:4).

I once preached an evangelistic crusade on the local ball field of a small town. On the first night, Jerald came forward at the invitation. Stinking, literally, of sin, he wept and cried out for mercy. Way more than half-crazy from drugs and alcohol, he wanted and needed restoration, not just forgiveness.

We gathered around Jerald and prayed, and somehow God reached him. Later as he walked down the street, vowing to be back, several of us watched his retreating form and waved away the fumes. His hair hung dank and oily to his shirtless shoulders. The shoeless feet that barely protruded from his ragged jeans were filthy beyond description. A red dragon with a dead baby in its talons was tattooed on his chest, and an eyeball with a dagger thrust in it was on his left shoulder blade.

"Now be honest," said one of the men. "Do you really believe even God can clean him up?"

I, too, doubted we'd ever see Jerald again. But we did. Again and again and again. He had never been in church before in his life, and now he seemed determined to make up for lost time. He was at every meeting, all the morning Bible classes and every pre-service prayer meeting. And each time he seemed a bit improved.

He had absolutely no idea how to act religious. One night when I arrived for the pre-service men's prayer meeting at the local church near the crusade ground, Jerald was already inside—alone in the dark—shouting at the top of his lungs.

"Jerald!" I demanded, as I flipped on the light. "What are you doing?"

Pausing in mid-stride, his face beaming, he waved his new Bible and cried out in sweet innocence, "Brother Mark, I'm in here just a-prayin' like h——!"

What does it mean that God in his mercy will put his name upon our foreheads? Does it mean a whitewashed vocabulary? Maybe. Maybe not. We need around us some tattooed saints fresh from the gutter. We get so saccharine in our rehearsed religiosity that it's a wonder heaven doesn't get diabetes just from listening to us pray. Jerald's prayers would have given no one diabetes. (Heart failure, maybe, but never diabetes.)

Restoration wants to stamp mercy's mark upon such a life that it may be clearly seen, not necessarily in pious utterances or the traditional trademarks we all know so well, but in life. When Jerald walked up the aisle that night on the ball field, he stank of death. But after the curse is broken and the Lamb comes to rule, the river that begins to flow out is not religion but *life*. That's what happened to Jerald.

What a glorious mercy it is that takes such a pagan and shines the light of Christ's life right out through his eyes. Only divine mercy would make God write his name on any of our faces. My face has been an advertisement for evil often enough. My eyes have certainly soaked up some twisted sights. Only mercy, and nothing else, would write God on *my* forehead.

Light from God

"The Lord God giveth them light" (Revelation 22:5).

A desperate call for help summoned my wife, Alison, to a mobile home. When Alison arrived she learned that the woman's husband had just confessed a "one-night stand" with some woman whose name he did not even know. It had happened long ago in a squandered and alcohol-soaked past, but for some reason, the wife was wounded afresh, as if it had just happened. She was devastated. The blackness of hurt and anger settled over her soul, and she doubted God's mercy to restore the light she had known.

She and Alison prayed together for hours, seeking a fresh revelation of the Cross. At times the woman seemed closer to a breakdown than a breakthrough. Suddenly, however, she began to receive insights beyond her experience. They flooded her with hope. She understood that Christ's forgiveness flowed through willing vessels. She was amazed that these thoughts would come to *her*. Light filled her dark mind and spirit.

"Oh, Alison," she cried out at last, "I ain't never been nobody like this before!"

In a similar way, darkness has settled heavily upon our society today. Frightened people search for light, any faint hope of light, that can make them feel a bit less alone and afraid and confused.

This longing for light is the basis of all cults and the occult. It is a search for some special insight on the Bible that only they have; a multicolored ray of light from under the doorway of the supernatural; or just some theory that makes the followers feel unique, enlightened and not so lost in the darkness. Whether found in a séance with crystals and pixie dust from Shirley MacLaine's own table or in an understanding of the "true" meaning of certain numbers in the Bible, the point is the pursuit. To know something, to see something that no one else can see except the elite whose eyes have been opened, that is the prize they seek.

Those who believe themselves thus enlightened are among the more dangerous folks in the world and in the church. Their "light" on the subject is all they have to make them able to bear the darkness. Just disturb it even the tiniest bit, dare to suggest that what they thought was the sunshine of a new revelation is nothing more than a penlight with a AAA battery, and you will learn what the children of darkness are capable of. Pilate hammered in the nails because Jesus dared to be a truth unknown in either pagan myth or his Roman sense of justice. A greater light than Pilate's own could not be borne.

It's a funny thing about the light of restoration. You wait for the floodlight to click on in a blaze of glory, but darkness gets gradually squeezed out until everything—not one thing, but literally *everything*—is seen differently.

Dominion with God
"And they shall reign" (Revelation 22:5).

Several years ago I got a clear picture of what this verse means. From where I stood in the doorway of a small Nigerian guest house, I could hear drums beating ominously. There was a witchcraft gathering in the place where an associate and I were to preach the next day, and some villagers were opposing the gospel with curses. We later learned that one of the senior fetish priests of the region had announced that we would not arrive alive at the platform.

The electricity was off where we were staying, so we ate our meal by lantern light in the stifling heat. As the eerie music grew a bit more raucous, I felt a shiver trying to get a toehold on my spine. The air was oppressive.

Suddenly I realized that my associate—a fine, sensitive young man in his twenties—was quietly leading our server to Christ. I had to chuckle. Those Nigerian witches, leaping and drumming in the night, had no power to keep a gentle, young child of God from stealing the strong man's goods right under his nose.

When Adam lost Eden, he also squandered the dominion he had enjoyed there. As steward-ruler of the garden, he brought everything in it under submission. Now that, too, was lost. From then on he must learn to make his way in a fallen universe where the prince of the power of the air ruled over legions of demons that hated Adam and all of his descendants. That was the new reality until Christ rose victorious, leaving Satan a defeated foe.

Today the battleground is in the individual life. Satanic forces bore into the flesh, build strongholds and hold on for dear death. The bondages of addiction and deception haunt the children of Adam. Most suicides are the result of forces of darkness never brought under dominion.

The final pearl of the five mercies of restoration is exactly that—dominion. To believe that Christ's blood forgives us our sins but that we are left to live out our lives in galling bondage is to believe a partial gospel that exchanges the mercy of God for universal defeatism. The Lamb wants to restore to us the dominion once lost. But what mercy to trust us again once confidence has been disappointed.

Now some have taken the concept of dominion too far by saying it means that having come into a faith relationship with Christ, we now have become as he is to reign in sovereign authority. Not only is this blasphemous, it would be sad if it were true. I am glad that mere humans, no matter how sanctified, do not rule the universe. What a nightmare! No one can be sanctified beyond the reach of stupidity and bad judgment. I do not want to think of the creative power of God in the tongue of a mortal.

The great truth is, we are not abandoned by God to live as powerless slaves to the elemental forces of the universe. "The name of the Lord is a strong tower; the righteous run to it and are safe" (Proverbs 18:10, NIV). In humility, not arrogance—hiding our will in his—we find that wonderful Adamic authority to rebuke temptations, spirits of darkness, satanic strongholds and tormenting bondage. This precious mercy of dominion restored is too little used by modern believers.

We have the authority of his name, not to order rain clouds about for selfish reasons or to call Cadillacs into our garages but to command until we rule those forces that have ruled us. This mercy of restoration comes gradually and with practice.

I interviewed a woman in Africa who had found great deliverance from spirits of confusion, darkness and depression. She had repented of a lifetime in witchcraft. For that, she was instantly forgiven. But the mercy of restoration is a process. She reported that every day had been a struggle at first. Sometimes she said she held her sanity by a fragile thread, screaming the name of Jesus at stubborn spirits of evil. Gradually, she said, she had grown in confidence, strength and authority. I could see it in her face. Her calm demeanor, radiant countenance and good-natured smile showed that dominion had been restored to her life.

"How long did it take?" I asked her.

"The first ten years were the hardest," she said. "Since then it has been easier. Still I grow."

Saints who will not go through the battle never build the muscles. No pain, no gain! "Still I grow," she said. *Yes, Lord,* I thought. *Be merciful to me, a sinner, and let me grow as well.*

The Dung Beetle

There was once a dung beetle named Lundquist. He lived on a farm in Minnesota and worked hard, keeping pretty much to himself. It's not that he was a driven workaholic like the ants. God forbid. Lundquist the dung beetle prided himself on knowing when to stop work and enjoy the fruits of his labors. It was just that he was earnest and dedicated. He was not obsessed, but he did take his work seriously.

One day Lundquist was rolling a particularly delightful ball along when some huge, powerful force squashed it flat as a pancake. Not easily defeated, Lundquist returned to the pasture and made himself another good-sized ball of dung. This he got only a tiny bit further when whatever it was returned and flattened this one as well. This time

Lundquist himself barely escaped.

This happened repeatedly until by the end of the day Lundquist was frustrated and discouraged. He looked at the eight balls of dung smashed into the dust, and he just wanted to cry. *I must be doing something wrong*, he thought. *These are all being destroyed in about the same place.* He did not know what to do. In his entire career he had never even considered quitting. Now he thought about it. *What is the use anyway? It is obviously never going to work.* He was a failure, a ne'er-do-well who couldn't roll dung balls any better than a rock badger.

Lundquist just dropped and closed his eyes against the sight of the eight pancakes that testified of his poor work. He was still lying like that when a Japanese beetle called to him from a tree limb overhead.

"*Ohi-oh*," said the Japanese beetle, and bowed.

"No," said Lundquist glumly. "Minnesota."

"No, no," the Japanese beetle responded, "*O-hi-oh* mean good morning in my language."

"Oh," said Lundquist, wondering why in the world anyone thought a dung beetle from Minnesota would understand Japanese. "Hello."

"What matter?" asked the Japanese beetle.

"Well, I'm not having a very good day," Lundquist replied, but he did not like this nosy foreigner. You didn't hear Lundquist saying, *Hey, why can't you speak English correctly? We don't poke our noses into other beetles' business in Minnesota.*

"What wrong?"

"Well, you can see I'm just not getting past this point," Lundquist said, pointing at the eight disasters. "I get to here, and the same thing happens every time."

The Japanese beetle looked at the flattened dung balls and saw the prints of tire treads. These he recognized as being from the huge green John Deere he could see chugging off toward the barn. The situation was clear to the Japanese beetle from where he sat. The farmer had been plowing and rolled his tractor over the dung balls at the end of each row.

"I think I'll just quit," Lundquist admitted, astonished at being so open with this stranger.

"Wrong!" cried the Japanese beetle, sounding oddly like John MacLaughlin. "You not quit now!"

"No?" Lundquist asked. "Why not?"

"This time you make it," said the Japanese beetle. "Try one more time. Go! Make new ball and come again. You not fail now!"

Somehow Lundquist found encouragement in the foreigner's commanding confidence. Yes, by jimminy, he would try again! Amazingly, this time he made it. No monstrous power destroyed his work. He was grateful to the Japanese beetle and told him so.

"Thanks, fella," Lundquist said. "You came along at just the right moment. I suppose that's some of that Oriental philosophy, huh?"

"No," said the foreign beetle. "Simple reality. Remember, when you got your nose in the dung, one above you can see the whole field."

Seven

Keeping Mercies

Velma was a willowy, frail-looking woman who somehow found the strength to bear a virtually impossible burden. She and her husband, Philip, made a meager living by piecing together his salary as a janitor and her wages as a part-time maid at a small nursing home. Their modest house was neat enough, but the cheap furniture had gone beyond threadbare and right on into shabby, without any hope of being replaced.

All seven of Velma and Phil's kids were still at home when I knew them. Seventeen-year-old Buddy wanted to be a mechanic, and Sissy, the baby, just wanted to be held. In between these two extremes were five others, including Sandra, who was wheelchair-bound. How Velma and Phil managed to feed them all was beyond me, but when winter came everybody seemed to have a coat of some sort, and though nobody but Buddy ever got anything new, they were all clean.

With this brood, and a house without modern conveniences, Velma worked like a dog, but I never heard her complain. In fact, she and Phil were not big talkers. But every Sunday morning they would be in church, occupying the same two pews.

One Sunday we had a guest singer. Between songs she would toss off one-liners about faith, then thrust a manicured index finger in the air and admonish us to "expect a miracle!"

I appreciated Velma's comment on the concert: "There's a whole lot of days when a miracle just won't do. Miracles only work once. I need something every day of my life."

"I know you do, Velma," I assured her.

"His mercies never come to an end," she said with a surprising passion in her eyes. "They are new every morning."

I agree with Velma. I also believe in miracles. I have seen them. They are a great act of mercy. Those who have dismissed miracles from the scene are premature. God is still God, and the mercy of a miracle is a joy to behold.

However, it is important to remember that on a day-to-day basis, the mercies of God, which are new every morning, are what we need when a miracle just won't do.

WHEN A MIRACLE JUST WON'T DO

God gives us another kind of mercy; I call it God's keeping mercy. It's the strength to get up and go again when all our power to do so is gone. Sometimes nothing will work but a miracle. But in those inglorious moments of sameness and tedium—when common ordinary people must live their lives without the extremes of heroic suffering or spectacular achievement, when nothing about their lives seems new—the keeping mercies of God are new every morning. The glamour of a miracle is a shot in the arm right when it's needed. Even greater is that quiet mercy that floods the exhausted and the war-weary and empowers them, against the onslaught of fatigue and fear and discouragement, to shoulder their packs and march one more painful mile.

That morning-by-morning mercy—Velma's kind of mercy—never gets much press, but it is requested plenty. Infinitely more people cry out to make it through today than cry out for a miracle. It's just that miracles make better headlines.

It would be a mistake, however, to comprehend the daily mercy of God as nothing more than grim endurance. Keeping mercy gives joy, even when there is little to be happy about. Some of the most fulfilled and, how shall I say it, *complete* persons I've ever known never got the miracle I wanted for them. I think, at least on some level, they also wanted the same miracle. Instead they found the faithfulness of God and mercies that never came to an end.

A dear friend of mine, Fran, is in heaven now. Her little body, so badly twisted in this life, is now in its glorified form. Having spent her mortality in the agonizing steel womb of a wheelchair, Fran has now been birthed into immortality. Whatever mobility looks like in heaven, it must be sweet indeed to Fran. Her father died before she did, in part just worn out from lifting her from wheelchair to van and out again. He must be enjoying watching her move about in a glorified body.

I longed to see Fran healed by a miracle. It seemed obvious to me that such a miracle would glorify God and be a blessing to the faith of many. But the miracle never came. I will not pretend that I understand or that it went the way I wanted. Why no miracle? I don't know.

What I do know is that in Fran *and* her dad I found a level of merciful joy beyond any I have seen in myself. Far from bedraggled, Fran's spirit was buoyant and joyful. She was good-humored and affirmative about life. Yes, heaven must be wonderful for her, but she never gave the appearance of waiting for it. Eternal life was, in her misshapen little body, a fountain of mercy.

Daily she sat behind the microphone of a local Christian radio station, praying for the needs of others. Many, perhaps most, who called in for Fran's "on the air" prayer time never knew that the exuberant voice of faith claiming *their* miracle belonged to the victim of a merciless birth defect. From her poured the Calvary love and sweet compassion of one who woke up every morning to two huge realities: horrible pain and the brand-new mercies of a faithful God.

If I had it to do over again, and God would let me choose, I know in my carnal mind that I would still take the miracle. I often wish I had seen Fran leap from that wheelchair. And I will not stop praying for miracles. Not ever! We should expect a miracle! But sometimes a miracle just won't do.

God's wide mercy has no end of blessing. His mercy upon the lost is wide enough to pay the full price of their redemption. He gives the Holy Spirit to those Christians who have discovered their inability to live the life of faith. The mercy of a miracle is a marvelous thing. But the mercy to make it through the day; the strength for the journey; the ability to endure the unendurable with joy unspeakable and full of glory; the mercy to make it through the long dark night of loneliness and depression and wait without panic for dawn to break—that mercy, that day-to-day mercy, is the one most of us need most of the time.

WHERE IS GOD WHEN IT HURTS?

The problem, of course, is that when we are suffering, we are not sure what God is feeling. It's one thing to say he is working out some long-range, redemptive purpose in my life. But what about now? Today I'm weeping. Where is God in that?

I suspect that one of the reasons God gives us kids is so we will know how he feels. Think how we feel in the painful crises of our children's lives. I believe it is a mistaken view of God that sees him as being emotionless in his choices. We believe in a God who speaks into our lives out of his own sovereign will. In one life a miracle. In another, daily struggle in the crucible of the unresolved. But how does it make God feel when we, his children, feel what we do at his decisions?

Dr. David Seamands and his wife, Helen, were well established in Indian missions when their baby Steve was born with a deformed foot. Advised by physicians that the defect needed a surgery best done in the United States, they left their beloved India. The hard part, however, lay ahead. Following surgery, Dr. Seamands had to do painful home therapy with the small boy. These excruciating exercises had to be done for the boy to ever walk normally. Dr. Seamands recounts how he would press on with them even as the boy screamed in agony. The father would soon be weeping as hard as the boy, but the painful process went on.

That seems to me a perfect picture of a God so merciful that he weeps with us in our pain but will not stop the process of our perfection. He keeps on relentlessly working, massaging the deep tissue of us, but he is not aloof from our emotions. As his thumbs dig in to knead our unresponsive flesh, we scream in pain, "Stop! Please stop! Have mercy on me."

"This is my mercy," comes the Father's reassuring voice. "I'm sorry it hurts, but to stop and leave you as crippled as you are would be merciless indeed."

In our agony we find this scant comfort and even doubt the goodness of a Father whose strong hands torture us so cruelly. Then we look up to see his gentle face wet with tears.

We must remember Christ in the cemetery with Mary and Martha at the funeral of their brother, Lazarus. Jesus did not chide them for weeping. Nor did he laugh at their tears because he knew he was on his way to raise up the one for whom they mourned. Jesus wept. He wept because they wept. The grandeur of his plan does not make his compassion in our pain any the less.

Annie Johnson Flint's body was also crippled like Fran's. Twisted by relentless arthritis, this anointed poet had to dictate her work to a friend. Unable to walk or even to hold a pen in her gnarled fingers, she nonetheless gave the community of faith an enduring inheritance of hope for daily mercy.

He giveth more grace
When the burden grows greater;
He sendeth more strength
When the labors increase.
To added affliction
He addeth His mercy
To multiplied trials, His multiplied peace.

When we have exhausted
Our store of endurance,
When our strength is gone
Ere the day is half done,
When we reach the end
Of our hoarded resources
Our Father's full giving is only begun.

His love has no limit;
His grace has no measure;
His pow'r has no boundary known unto men.
For out of His infinite riches in Jesus,
He giveth
And giveth
And giveth again.[1]

GOD'S MERCIES COME IN DIFFERENT WAYS

Balance is the most difficult of all theological disciplines.
It is tempting to go "right to the wall" on one theological
conviction or another without allowing it to be tempered
where needed. It is merciless to steal from the afflicted all

hope of a miracle with a phrase like, "God doesn't do that anymore."

On the other hand, there are those who, in their affliction, need a merciful church to embrace with them the keeping mercies of God. To reprimand the afflicted for some presumed lack of faith is as reprehensible as denying them all hope for a miracle.

God's mercies never fail, but they come to us in different ways. The one who finds the mercy of a miracle needs no other. But the downtrodden—to whom the keeping mercy does not lift their burden but sustains their spirit—need mercy all around. God does the choosing. He is sovereign. But we also must be merciful to one another, rejoicing in miracles and hefting one another's loads. Let the people of God show mercy, even as he does.

Whether one member suffer, all the members suffer with it; or one member be honored, all the members rejoice.

1 CORINTHIANS 12:26

The Ferry

Shafiq den Nasser was a farmer on the banks of the Nile. Every morning he would rise early, before dawn, to be in the field when the sun came up. He would pick enough produce to load his donkey and go into the city. There he sold his tomatoes and okra to the housewives and bought whatever supplies he needed. This he did every day but the Sabbath. He was not in poverty, but he lived day by day.

One day as he waited at the ford for the ferry to come back across, a young man dressed like a prince arrived. The young man peered across the wide river at the distant ferry. He fidgeted nervously, so Shafiq assumed he was in a hurry.

"That ferry moves very slowly," the young man said.

"Yes, *effendi*," Shafiq agreed. "Very slowly."

"Well, is there no faster way across? I am in a great hurry."

"Yes, *effendi*," Shafiq told him, "there is a faster way. Those men down there; you see them, yes, there. They can take you across in a small boat much faster. But I warn you they are much more expensive than the ferry."

"That's no problem," said the young prince. "Come, my good man, you shall ride with me. Let the ferry take your donkey. We will go on to the other side and have some coffee."

Shafiq was amazed at this offer. It was very kind. But he was concerned to leave the donkey and his produce for others to lead onto the ferry.

"*Effendi*," Shafiq said with a bow. "Thank you, but I cannot accept. You go on. I'll just wait for the ferry."

"Don't be foolish," laughed the rich man. "I'll pay. Why not ride in luxury for once in your life?"

"Thank you," Shafiq said. "But I'll take the ferry. A fancy ride is fine for you. You only need to get across today. I must cross the river every single day. The ferry never fails. You won't be here tomorrow or the next day or the next."

The rich man left, and soon Shafiq could see him speeding across the river in a beautiful boat with cushions for him to lie on. He waved gaily to Shafiq and soon was gone.

Finally the ferry came and unloaded its passengers. Shafiq led the donkey on board and tied him to a rail just where he did every day. Then, just as he did every day, he went up to stand by the ferryman who was his friend.

"Well, Shafiq," the ferryman hailed him. "How are you this morning?"

"Fine, Ali," Shafiq answered. "And you?"

"I'm fine also," the ferryman answered, beginning to pull on the wet rope. "The sun is not as hot today. Thank God for small mercies."

"Yes," Shafiq said. "Small mercies are the best for poor men and donkeys."

"Blessed are the merciful, for they shall obtain mercy."

MATTHEW 5:7

Eight

Mercy for Life

"My son would never lie to me," proclaimed the fuming man in my office.

"Mine might," I offered with a chuckle.

He gasped. "Look, you and I obviously have very different views of childrearing."

"Ah," I assured him, "that's where I suspect you're wrong. We just have different views of children. I think that the best kid alive today might lie, under the right circumstances, and do it convincingly."

"Not mine!" he announced again, and I thought I heard it thunder.

The parent who says, "My child will never …" is merciless to the child. What that parent is saying, in effect, is, "The child I love, the one whom I am willing to claim, is *perfect* in this respect." It is not the true child—with all his or her sins and lacks and lies intact—that is loved. Some other child, some perfectly truthful, perfectly behaved, perfectly wonderful Little Lord Fauntleroy is adored. The child who fits that description shall be loved, but woe to the child if he or she falls short. What a burden for a child to carry!

This is not just about how we view kids, it's about how we view LIFE. The people who believe their kids would never lie may also believe their cars will never break down, their pastor will never disappoint them and the check is in the mail. But life in an imperfect, fallen universe is chockfull of imperfect falls.

For the world and for life, we need the mercy of reality. We must embrace this imperfect world not with that malignant cynicism, which is idealism gone wrong, but with balance and grace and humor. There are mountains and there are molehills. Mrs. James' boys, Jesse and Frank, played with guns and had this thing for banks. *That* is a mountain. But even that, *even that* does not necessarily mean the end of parental hope and joy and love. Your child gnaws her fingernails and blames it on the Easter Bunny? That is a molehill!

LIFE IS NOT ABOUT "GETTING IT RIGHT"

The merciless edge of perfectionism constantly cuts away at our perspective. It distorts life. It flattens and perverts perception until we view the universe against a single horizon of colorless, joyless judgmentalism. In such a world nothing is funny. No hues are mixed; nothing is ever grievous and grand and small, all at once. Everything is either all good or all bad, on the canvas or off; and all is of the same size.

Jesus did not demand that everything be perfect. He embraced people as they were, with all their sores and sins. Indeed, he mocked the sanctimonious. He not only denounced the pious pretenders, he also made them look just plain silly.

He mocked the Pharisees' prayer. "I thank you, God, that I am not as others are—weak, unjust, immoral dogs, whose kids will lie at school. I am disciplined, and my kids excel" (Luke 18:11, author's paraphrase).

Instead Jesus justified the poor guy in the back row who drove a beer truck and whose kid got kicked out of day care. What did Jesus mean? That it was good to drive a beer truck and rear undisciplined kids? No. What he meant was that just because such a lowly shoe fits us, he is not going to write us off, nor should we write off each other.

When I was young, I thought life was about getting all the knickknacks arranged on the shelf and then keeping them dusted. Trouble is, someone is always knocking everything off with a basketball, which he shouldn't have in the house anyway. Just when we get things perfect, something happens to mess it all up again.

But life is not about "getting it right." It's about walking in the grace of God when things are not all right. The mercies of God are new *every* morning, not just the perfect mornings. Mercy is new when my wife has just run the car into the garage door for the fifth time. It has to be! Mercy is new when my brother-in-law arrives to stay for a week, and when God in his infinite wisdom rains on my particular parade.

LIFE OFF THE HOOK

Life is not perfect. Kids are not, schools are not, spouses and houses and pastors and churches are not. If you spend your life hovering over your sacred knickknacks, fighting off all the flying B-balls, you will find yourself growing angrier and more brittle with people and with God.

I once passed a funeral home with a hearse parked out front for the imminent end of the service inside. Somber men in dark suits were opening the back door and trying to arrange themselves in two lines. But in the driveway two rowdy little boys in dress clothes were playing soccer with a soup can.

An elderly woman was laughing and shouting encouragement. In the heat her corsage had wilted and her hat was askew, but her joy in the fabric of life let children be children, even while someone her own age, perhaps a loved one, was being sent off to Glory. Was she their grandma? More probably a joyful aunt. She was in touch with the reality of life. Right now there was a soccer match that badly needed cheering on, and little boys with energy to be spent. The funeral inside was part of life. So was the soccer game in the driveway.

Some people may try to make a good-and-evil issue out of that, saying the boys should have been reprimanded because a funeral is no time for fun and games. I think God would disagree.

Where was God, you ask? Inside at the funeral, comforting the bereaved. And outside, laughing at the boys with the soup can.

The truly anxious of this world are not those who are worried about global warming or nuclear annihilation, but those who have finally got the house clean and dread the return of all the dirt trackers. The goal of Christian living is not to get it all together and then sit in terror, waiting for the other shoe to drop. Relax. It probably will drop just when it will do the worst damage. This is not mere pessimism, however.

A certain man who was reputed to be the worst pessimist in the world was asked, "Is that true? Are you the biggest pessimist in the world?"

"I'm afraid to admit it," the man answered. "It's probably illegal."

We will be made dismal and morbid by an imperfect world unless we can free it up to be as imperfect as it is, and free ourselves from the ultimate responsibility to tidy up. Does this sound like an invitation to be an irresponsible beach bum? Certainly not, but the beach bum can teach the perfectionist a few things about having a little mercy.

This admission that things and projects and people go awry should not put fear in our hearts. It should teach us to know that some things are to weep about, some to be laughed at, and may God give us the mercy to know which is which. There is precious little mercy in the world and in the church. For the perfectionist there is none at all.

There is a tragic pride in perfectionism. How dare my child disappoint, my husband go bankrupt, my hair turn gray. Forrest Gump was right about one thing, you never know what you're gonna get. But that's not the bad part. That's the good part! That is the adventure and the fun.

Tears will come. We will sustain griefs and hurts and wounds. That's life. The good, the bad and the ugly all go in together. My wife saw a tag on a dress that said,

"This fabric woven of natural fibers. The irregularities only serve to enhance the beauty of the garment."

Now set this book down and walk through your house or office, absolving offending imperfections. Look at that beat-up old Chevy in the driveway and absolve it for not being a Porsche. Do it. Actually raise your hand and say, "I absolve you." Say it to the toaster, to your husband's golf clubs and to your kid's messed-up room. Then look in the mirror and say it to yourself. Make a funny face and say it again. Then sit down and read the next chapter, and remember, "A merry heart doeth good like a medicine" (Proverbs 17:22).

Schoenberg's

The smells emanating from Bernie Schoenberg's deli were irresistible. Every time the door opened a rich aroma would waft out to the sidewalk and in would come some passerby who was suddenly starving to death. The salami and the big red onions by themselves were a bit strong. Bernie, who knew this of course, always kept them blended with the odors of dark pumpernickel bread and chicken soup bubbling in a huge pot, and coffee brewing on the stove. This filled the air inside Schoenberg's with a rich and rare perfume.

Bernie absolutely loved it when people came in and asked, "What is that wonderful smell?"

"Schoenberg's," he'd say with a laugh.

One customer would order a kosher hot dog and baked beans; another would call for baklava and European coffee. A certain old man from Krakow came in every Thursday for a quart of chicken soup and one dozen bagels. Every time, the old man said the same thing.

"That smell. My mother's kitchen. I tell you, Bernie, my mother's kitchen."

"I know," Bernie would say, and they would nod at each other as the elderly do when they share a secret not known by younger men.

One day a salesman from Schenectady came into Schoenberg's selling air fresheners guaranteed to eliminate odors and leave only a brisk pine scent. It was an industrial strength disinfectant, claimed the salesman, that could make a room smell clean and new. Anyway, he said, it was 20 percent off, and guaranteed.

"Whadda ya, crazy?" Bernie yelled. "Get outta here! This is not a cedar chest in your mother's attic! This is Schoenberg's! A deli with no odor except pine trees is unnatural."

"But isn't the pure, clean scent of— ?"

"Out! Out! Out, ya putz! This is Schoenberg's! I don't want a pure, clean smell! I want Schoenberg's!"

Nine

Mercy for Yourself

Many years ago, when I was a young pastor, I knew a fellow I'll call Harold. Harold had an alcohol problem, but I liked him and occasionally went fishing with him. He loved to laugh and absolutely delighted in making me laugh. He came to church several times a year, but always alone. His wife went every Sunday to another church.

When Harold died, his wife felt obliged to invite me to take part in his funeral, which was held at her church. Her pastor was in his late sixties, and he was not amused at having a twenty-five-year-old preacher on his platform—not even for the funeral of a drunk.

"Do you want to speak first or last?" he demanded, barely shaking my hand.

"Last, I guess."

"No!" he snapped. "You go first."

"Fine, sir," I agreed, wishing I were somewhere bass fishing.

In my eulogy, I talked about Harold's many kindnesses to me and made only an indirect reference to the "complications" of his life. I talked about Harold's great, good humor and saw heads nodding across the room. They obviously remembered the same quick, hearty laughter. I shared about a time Harold got a fishing lure stuck in his own earlobe and he had the grace to laugh about it.

The pastor was furious. He ranted and raved for twenty minutes, even turning to point his finger in my face and denounce "irreverent young men who tell jokes at funerals!" I was humiliated to say the least.

On the brief walk out to the graveside just behind the church, I asked the pastor if he wanted me to do anything there.

"No!" he snapped. "You've done quite enough already!"

I submitted eagerly to this, but he did not believe me and assertively walked to the head of the casket. But when he did, he plunged into the grave. The casket, suspended as it was on a sling, budged just far enough to let him slip in, then pinned him against the side of the grave. I slapped a hand over my mouth to keep from laughing while the two gravediggers cranked up the sling and Harold's coffin. They pulled the minister out of the grave, fuming and slapping at them, absolutely covered in wet, red clay.

I think I would have made it, but when the widow erupted in whoops of laughter, I was a goner. I just doubled over and laughed my head off. So did everyone else under that funeral tent.

The Lord spoke to me that day in the cemetery. He said two things that have informed the balance of my ministry. First of all, he said, look at this and learn. When you do a funeral, stand back from the grave. Second, if you do fall in, laugh first!

THERE'S ONLY ONE THING TO DO ...

Most people have a merciless expectation of themselves; they vow never to do or say anything outrageously stupid. Most of us learn the hard way that this is absolutely impossible—at least this has always been impossible for me.

I ran into an acquaintance I had not seen for some time, and after a few seconds of greetings, I asked, "Well, how's your wife?"

"Wonderful, I suspect," he replied softly. "She's in heaven where she has been for six months."

What does one do at such a moment? Suicide is an option, of course. Just drop to your knees right in front of the offended party and open your veins. Keep repeating, "I'm sorry, I'm sorry, I'm so, so sorry," as he watches you go on to be with his wife, where presumably you can spend eternity apologizing to her.

Or you can just add yet another memory to the ever-growing file of things you've done to make yourself feel like a donkey. Everyone has such a list. We try to forget the list. Suppression works in spurts, but sooner or later one of these painful memories will force itself onto the screen of our mental computer, reminding us of how utterly, abysmally, unforgivably stupid we are. That one incident (and remember, there's a file full) was sufficient to prove it.

There's only one cure: cultivate the ability to laugh at yourself. This is the mercy of mirth. Those who do not learn to laugh at themselves are doomed to merciless self-condemnation. A sense of humor insulates us against the blows of life. And a sense of humor is not knowing what's funny, it's knowing what's funny about you.

One year, at our annual youth convention, a wonderful kid named Ian showed five hundred dreadfully serious-about-themselves teens how to laugh at life's tragedies. Ian, who was born with only one leg, wore a sophisticated but strange-looking prosthesis. The first time I saw him in shorts, I knew that this handsome, calm young man was not at all insecure about his leg. But when he put the leg on backwards in the boys' dorm and ran with the artificial foot facing to the rear, he brought the house down. Suddenly Ian plunged to the floor, grabbing the "ankle" of the prosthetic device as he howled in pain.

"I sprained my ankle!" he cried in agony. "Help me up, please. I sprained my ankle."

Two boys tenderly lifted him to his feet as he winced at the painful sprain. Only when he winked did we realize that, of course, a person cannot sprain an artificial ankle! It nearly caused a riot of relieved laughter.

The really sad people in life are merciless with themselves, demanding mistake-free, idiot-proof, physically, mentally and spiritually perfect living. We mortals must have mercy. Psalm 103:14 says that God "knoweth our frame; he remembereth that we are dust." If God can remember that, shouldn't we? Shouldn't we cut ourselves some slack and learn to laugh at our failures and foul-ups along the way? Have a little mercy on yourself.

In another of my early churches was an eccentric widow and her sixtyish maiden daughter; everyone called them the Raffield girls. They were a couple of the oddest old things you'd ever want to meet. But they knew it, and found themselves and their lives a hoot.

Old Mrs. Raffield had false teeth that she would let slip, then clack back into place loudly. The effect lent an amazing animation to everything she said. Billie Jean, the daughter, never said a word, but found her mother's stories a source of unending amusement. She would stand at her mother's elbow, nodding and smiling, as she eagerly awaited the punch line, then burst into infectious gales of laughter.

"Why don'tcha come out to the house and visit us?" Mrs. Raffield clacked one Sunday.

"How about tomorrow?" I said.

"Fine! Only stay in the car till I come out to get you. I've gotta dog named Big Boy. Some folks will tell ya their dog won't bite. Big Boy'll kill ya!"

Indeed, the creature was the Hound of the Baskervilles! It was part Rottweiler, part Doberman and altogether demon-possessed.

One Sunday the Raffield girls came to church carrying a white cane and a pair of heavy men's sunglasses. These Billie Jean carried out in front of her like wet galoshes.

"Well," Mrs. Raffield said, beaming. "Big Boy can heal the sick."

"The dog?" I asked, thinking he could more likely make a meal of them.

"Yep," she said with an exceptionally loud clack. "The hand o' God is on him. He's anointed. He can make the blind to see and the deaf to hear. Big Boy's a miracle worker. Yesterday a blind man tapped up our walk with this cane and knocked on the door. He handed me a card that said he was a Vietnam vet that had been left blind and deaf by the war and could I give him some money. Well, while I was fishin' in my purse, Big Boy came a shootin' past and hit the screen door a snarlin' and growlin' like you seen him do. Well, preacher, that man tore off them glasses, dropped this white cane here and ran off as healed as can be. Now ain't that a miracle?"

Mrs. Raffield knew the mercy of mirth. She could have gone on about how terrible the world is getting, and let the incident fuel her suspicions of people, but instead she chose to laugh and help others laugh by telling the story. Because she chose to laugh, her load was lighter, and so was mine.

LAUGHTER LIGHTENS THE LOAD

Life is full of things that are too difficult to bear and too funny not to laugh about.

A missionary made his way home to South Carolina sick and weary. The combination of parasites, foreign food and a rough flight over the Pacific had just about done him in. Then from Los Angeles to Dallas he was seated by the window with a large, stinking drunk between him and the aisle. The drunken man fell asleep with his mouth open and his head tilted sideways. His fetid breath was the last straw. Suddenly, and with very little warning, the missionary vomited all over the sleeping passenger who, despite the drenching, failed to awaken. Using his hanky, the missionary cleaned his own mouth, turned his face to the window and waited. In a few seconds the man awoke and stared in horror at the nightmare in his lap.

"Oh, my!" he shouted.

"There now," the missionary said, patting the man's arm comfortingly. "Don't you feel better?"

Learning to laugh at ourselves restores the perspective to laugh at life. There is great mercy in that. Take everything with the same level of seriousness, and you will crack.

A charismatic pastor in the South told me that he had a guest evangelist in to preach for a few nights. A certain woman, who considered herself a prophetess, did not like the visiting preacher and told the pastor that the Lord had revealed to her that the meetings should be canceled and the guest sent packing. When the pastor refused, she knew she had to act.

The next night, just as the evangelist began speaking, she leapt to her feet and, pointing her finger in his face, wailed out her "word of prophecy."

"Thus saith the Lord," she cried. "Thou thinkest thou art a humdinger. But thou art not a humdinger! Thou art a dinger!"

The pastor and his congregation were horrified. No one knew what to do until the evangelist burst out laughing. The pastor first, then the congregation, caught the cue until laughter like latter-day rain filled the whole building. The woman was so miffed and her pride was so wounded that she left, flouncing up the middle aisle.

I like that story. Some things don't deserve to be treated with dignity. A merry heart doeth good like medicine, and that night an entire congregation got free, for a while at least, of religious pretension and spiritual gamesmanship.

There is one thing, though. It's kind of funny, but in one way that woman was right. It's a word of prophecy we all need. "Thou thinkest that thou art a humdinger, but thou art a dinger." You are a dinger. Set yourself free from the need to be a humdinger in a world full of dingers. You're a dinger, too. But it's all right. It's even funny when you can see it. Have a little mercy on yourself. Thou art a dinger!

Mr. President

It was a Norman Rockwell print, and Robert Fishbein knew it. The president of the United States eating ice cream in the Oval Office with his grandson. A picture of this would be worth a hundred thousand votes. He considered calling for the White House photographer but decided against it. There really wasn't time. The president was within minutes of making the most important speech of his career. It was probably for the best anyway. The folksy little scene might look frivolous in light of the seriousness of this issue.

"Mr. President," he said gravely.

"Yes, Bob."

"It's about time," Fishbein reminded him. "Don't

you think?" he said, nodding meaningfully at the seven-year-old slurping ice cream from a china bowl.

"Yeah, yeah," sighed the president. "Look, Collin. I guess you better go on upstairs now. I'll call Mrs. Rodriguez to come and get you. I'll be right there, Bob."

As the White House chief of staff went out, closing the door silently behind him, Collin studied his grandfather's face for a moment, then tossed the spoon loudly into the empty bowl.

"Grandpa," he asked. "Are you sad?"

"No, Collin," the president said, straightening his tie. "Not sad exactly. Just serious, I guess. I'm under a lot of stress right now. But you don't need to think about that. There's nothing you can do unless you'd like to make this speech for me."

The president looked at his grandson and flashed the boy a wan smile. "Anyway, the speech won't wait. How do I look?"

"Your pants are unzipped," said the boy.

The president gasped, bending to clutch at his trousers. They were not unzipped.

"Made you look, you dirty crook. Stole your mother's pocketbook. Turned it in, turned it out, turned it into sauerkraut!" laughed the boy.

"Why, you ..." the president shouted and grabbed for his grandson, who nimbly danced out of reach.

The door opened again, and Fishbein and Mrs.

Rodriguez were there, looking like pallbearers.

"It's time, sir," Fishbein said softly. "Mrs. Rodriguez will take Collin."

Grandfather and grandson kissed good-bye, and each started in different directions with his own keeper. Just at the door of the White House press room, the president paused and whispered to the chief of staff.

"Bob, your fly's open."

"Oh, my ..." Fishbein gasped, then added, "No, it's not."

"Made you look, you dirty crook!"

Ten

Mercy for Your Family

One of my favorite movies is *Arsenic and Old Lace.* I love watching Cary Grant mug it up when he finds a dead body in the window seat. I howl with laughter when he screams at one elderly man to keep him from drinking poisoned wine. And I smile knowingly as the dull-witted cop on the beat decides he absolutely *must* tell the plot of his play, despite the fact that there are at least four homicidal maniacs in the house. But most of all I think of how the imperfections of Mortimer Brewster's family haunt him.

Mortimer Brewster is the critic played by Cary Grant. A confirmed bachelor, he writes with acidity on the subject of marriage, at least until he himself falls in love—if not with the girl next door, then at least with the girl across the cemetery. Surely you remember the story.

Mortimer and his fiancée procure a marriage license, then stop by their houses, she to pack and he to say good-bye to the two sweet old aunties who raised him. He discovers that for some time the two old darlings have been poisoning lonely old men and burying them in the basement, with the help of their brother, who believes himself to be Teddy Roosevelt. It is this same Uncle Teddy who sounds a bugle and screams "Charge!" every time he climbs the stairs, as though he were attacking San Juan Hill.

Just at this time, Mortimer's older brother, a monstrous serial killer, arrives with Peter Lorre and a dead body of his own. Poor Mortimer now sees that it is impossible for him to pass on the murderous genes so obviously swimming around in the Brewster pool.

He breaks off his engagement and sets about getting the brother out of the house, and his two aunties and Uncle Teddy into a nearby insane asylum.

The denouement comes as Mortimer prepares to sign as "the next of kin." The two old girls draw him aside and tell him the "dreadful truth." He is not, they explain, a Brewster at all. In fact, he was the child of their maid and the cook from a tramp steamship. As soon as the baby was born, the maid absconded, leaving the two sisters to raise Mortimer.

"You mean I'm not a Brewster?" he asks.

"No, Mortimer," one of the aunts mutters, "you're not."

At this Mortimer crows triumphantly and dashes next door to inform his fiancée of the great news.

"I'm not a Brewster!" he shouts. "I'm not a Brewster! I'm the son of a sea cook!"

When we survey the antics and sins of our families, there is from time to time in each of us the faint hope that just in the nick of time we will find out we were left on the doorstep by gypsies.

THERE ARE NO PERFECT FAMILIES

No family is perfect. Absolutely *no family* is perfect. Locked away out of sight, in some inner vault, lie the skeletal remains of all we wish we could forget. On even the finest of family trees grow some strange limbs. You will never perfect your family, but you can learn to have mercy on them.

Yet, knowing this, we still harken to the cold, harsh voice of the law. I heard one renowned family teacher say that if we would all show him what's wrong with our teens, he would gladly show us what we did wrong. What a preposterous idea! God himself raised Adam in the only perfect environment, and Adam still sinned. What did God do wrong? I am not saying we have no responsibility in our families. Nor am I saying that we do not have negative and positive influence. But I do mean to say that if you attempt to draw a direct cause-and-effect line between every weakness, sin or defect in your children and some negative parenting pattern in your life, you will go nuts.

Have mercy on yourself and your kids. You are not the ultimate cause of every sin your children commit nor of every dumb decision they ever make. Your children have a God-given, inalienable, theological right to their own sins. Cut yourself some slack.

Legalism's claim that every action has a corresponding cause is untrue and unnecessarily damning. Life is complex. Families and folks are complicated. And sometimes people we love make the most incredibly stupid and destructive decisions. Surely we will grieve. But at some point the umbilical cord of parental responsibility must be tied off and snipped. I often tell teens to look at their navel. That, I say, means you are now on your own. That tiny little knot is there to remind you that from here on your decisions are on your own head. Quit blaming Mom and Dad.

FREEDOM FROM THE NEED TO BE PERFECT

Familial mercy liberates. First of all, it frees us from being enslaved to the appearance of perfection. If every family has problems, then why am I working so hard to keep my neighbors from finding out about mine?

I was preaching in a college town when a young couple spoke to me after a service. They had been married less than a year and were already in serious trouble. They were sexually and relationally dysfunctional, and they knew they needed help.

"Why haven't you gone for counseling?" I demanded.

Her father was a local pastor and his was a high-profile faculty member, and they were terrified that someone might know the awful truth—that they were human! They had cut themselves off from lines of support because they were trying to live under the merciless lash of public image.

They are not alone in their fear. Another couple left their church home because their only daughter turned to drugs. Rather than lean on friends who had been supportive, they found a huge church where no one knew them—a place where they blended in with the woodwork. When they needed mercy the most, their fear of being "found out" forced them out of a loving community church. How sad.

And what is true for the congregation is also true for the pastor. Just as lay people should be freed from the expectation of perfection, so should pastors. Merciless and legalistic congregants announce to already hurting parents in ministry, "Your child is in sin, therefore your own house is not in order. Resign!"

When we are honest about our own imperfections, how can we show anything but mercy? The church is made up of imperfect families. There are the Smiths. Their daughter got pregnant before she got married. And there are the Brownstones. Jimmy got arrested for shoplifting. And the Butlers and the Roths and all the rest who need mercy from God and each other much more than high-handed sermons on how they've messed up their kids.

FREEDOM FROM PERFECTING OTHERS

Freed from slavery to appearances we can set ourselves free of the need to "perfect" anyone else. You are not the other members of your family. You need not live in shame for what others have done. Likewise, you cannot live out your life through the lives of others.

Parents want to take pride in the accomplishments and successes of their children, but sometimes that pride becomes a destructive projection. If we are not ultimately to blame for our children's sins, then we cannot claim some ultimate role as bestower of all their gifts. That is God's job.

Yes, it's fine to see and even point out that little Sally has detached earlobes just like old Uncle Wally, or that Grandpa and baby Tim are the only "outies" in a family full of "innies." But you just dare to lean over that cradle daily and mutter the mantra of "be a doctor, be a doctor," and at some point little Sally and tiny Tim may explode in lethal rebellion.

Let me repeat, you are not defined by the imperfections in your family. So what if Aunt Margaret thinks she's a kumquat, or if cousin Bill got lost somewhere in the seventies and keeps appearing at family gatherings dressed like Austin Powers and handing out packs of free marijuana cigarettes autographed by Timothy Leary? So what? Every family in town has a few loonies in a closet somewhere.

You are who you are. That's final! The cavalry is not going to ride in at the last moment with the news that you don't belong to this weird bunch of knuckleballs. Even if you are adopted, the lot who birthed you are certainly as zany as the ones who reared you. Nope. Nobody is exempt. Your family tree has just as many knotholes as everyone else's, but you are not your family, and your kids are not you. Too many Christians spend their lives in useless embarrassment over their ancestors or their kids.

Release your family to be different, complicated and wrong. Set them free to fail, to learn by experience and to suffer hardships. The parents of the prodigy gloat while the parents of the rebel sulk. Have mercy on yourself, and your kith and kin, by realizing that no family is perfect. Quit taking your relations so seriously, and stop—please STOP!—wearing that successful kid like a diamond stickpin, or your troublesome one like an albatross.

FREEDOM FROM FINISHING

A word of mercy, as well, for the parents of young adults. You do not have to "finish" your kids. You do the best you can in the time you have, and then you let time, girlfriends, wives and drill sergeants finish 'em off. What you could not, absolutely *not* get your son to stop, he will quit at the very first complaint from a girl he has fallen for head over heels.

You've been trying to get your daughter to quit spending so much money on long distance calls, and she will not listen to you. Right? Then along comes her white knight with a minimum wage job, and they want to get married. Let *him* convince her. As they drive off in a borrowed car for a two-day honeymoon, don't weep. Laugh the laughter of mercy and remember she's his job now. Hallelujah! Let him change her.

Your family is not perfect. The only perfect family is mine. My perfect kids have wrecked cars, gone through colleges like Grant went through Richmond and reminded entire congregations why they made up all those jokes about preachers' kids. But they are, after all, mine and I love them, not despite their imperfections but *in* their imperfections. Every little crack and flaw is precious to me. I refuse to be so merciless to them and to myself as to hate their imperfections as reflecting badly upon me. Neither will I steal their successes from them by claiming them as the fruit of my great parenting. Both would be merciless indeed.

Norman McLean's great book *A River Runs Through It* is the brilliant account of a Montana pastor and his two rowdy sons. The elder boy, the book's author, becomes a college professor and an author. But the younger son wastes his life in alcohol and gambling until he is finally beaten to death for an unpaid debt.

The Reverend McLean, in his last recorded sermon, proclaimed that we are often unable to reach those in our families who need us the most. We may never understand them. We may never help them. But we can, by the mercies of God, love them and forgive them, and in the process forgive ourselves as well.

Mayor of Quang Zi

The army of General Po wound like a giant dragon around the hillocks and down through the valley of the River Chang. The general rode at its head like a ferocious beast of prey, and behind him, in a covered sedan chair carried by eight massive slaves, was his daughter PuLi.

No one had ever seen PuLi, but she was reputed to be the most beautiful woman in the world. So lovely was General Po's daughter, in fact, that whenever she was to appear, even for a second, the entire army had to fall on their faces and close their eyes. All of her ladies-in-waiting had their tongues cut out so that having seen her they could not describe her beauty to anyone.

Many men had risked their lives for only a glimpse of her. Many had died. None had actually seen her and lived. So the legend of her beauty grew, even as did the cruelty of her father's conquests.

General Po was the greatest of all the warlords, and the path behind his army was a wake of death and destruction. Every town, every village was remorselessly sacked and burned. And each time the great general would pronounce the same judgment "Unworthy! You are unworthy!"

Word of this quickly spread so that each village and town made more extravagant preparations than the last, hoping to impress General Po and the lovely PuLi. The poor were driven away, the lame and the halt were either hidden from view or slain, the buildings were painted and the most exquisite decorations imaginable were hung in the streets. The town's most beautiful girls would strew flower petals under the hooves of the general's horse, and the strongest and most handsome youths would line the roads, holding gifts of inestimable value. The elderly, the weak and the ugly were sent into the hills, and only the best and the most beautiful were presented to General Po's eyes. But each time it was in vain. Each time the merciless warlord would proclaim the unworthiness of the place and then destroy it utterly.

The last village in the valley was the poorest one of all. Quang Zi was hardly more than a cluster of huts and a few ramshackle buildings. The peasants of Quang Zi were hard workers, but their fields were poor and rocky. Their lives were meager and desperate, but still they did not want to be slaughtered by the army of General Po.

"What shall we do?" they cried. "Even the most beautiful cities in the valley were unworthy. What can we do?"

"Nothing," said the mayor.

"What!?" they wailed. "You mean give up hope?"

"No," said the mayor. "Never that. But do nothing. We cannot make ourselves worthy with paper streamers and gifts of peacock feathers. We are who we are."

"Yes," said the peasants of Quang Zi. "That is right. We are who we are."

The next morning when the great General Po rode into Quang Zi, he was astonished at what he saw. There were no preparations for his arrival. No lanterns were hung, no damsels danced and no singers sang of his greatness. Only the mayor and his son came out to greet him. General Po reined in his horse and glared down at the humble man before him.

"You are welcome," said the mayor, bowing low. "Quang Zi is yours. We are not rich. We are not powerful. We are humble farmers. But we greet you in peace."

Beside the mayor stood his son. This young man had a terrible scar across his face. Many in the village wished that the mayor had left him in the house. The scar was actually a gruesome disfigurement.

"Who is that?" demanded General Po.

"This is my son," the mayor answered.

"What is wrong with his face?" the great general asked, peering down at the hapless boy from astride his stallion.

"He had an accident," the mayor explained. "When he was a boy he would not listen to me, and he tried to use a tool that was too strong for him. But he has learned his lesson, and I am very proud of him. Very proud! He is a fine son."

At this General Po dismounted and embraced the mayor.

"Come," said the general. "Ride on my horse."

And he led the little mayor of Quang Zi through the town like an emperor. The boy with the scarred face was invited to ride with the princess in her sedan chair, and later they were married.

Even on her wedding day she wore a veil. But the groom was visible to everyone.

Eleven

Mercy and Forgiveness

Many years ago I taught a fourth-grade Sunday school class in Maryland. I learned more about church life from those kids than I did in seminary.

One Sunday I had just finished a lesson on turning the other cheek when I stepped out into the hallway and found one of the girls weeping piteously.

"Melanie," I said, dropping to one knee, "what in the world has happened?"

"Jeremy hit me!" she wailed.

"He just walked up to you and hit you? Why would he do that?"

"No," she blubbered. "I hit him first."

"But why, Melanie? Why would you do that?"

"I asked him," she explained through her sobs, "if he believed what you taught about turning the other cheek. When he said yes, I slapped him. And he hit me back!"

I know how she felt. I want everybody else to act like a Christian.

I could be a saint if I lived on a deserted island. It's other people's Christianity that makes a mess of mine. The real crucible of faith is that place of heated friction where our lives rub up against the lives of others. The law is this: the broader the surface of contact, the greater the friction generated. In other words, a stranger may irritate you, but not like your cousin does. Cousins can freak you out at the annual family reunion, but a brother can make you crazy every week. The boss can do it daily, but nobody can drive you totally, completely up the wall like your wife and kids.

"Yea, mine own familiar friend," David lamented, "in whom I trusted, who did eat of my bread, hath lifted up his heel against me" (Psalm 41:9).

The wounds of a stranger do not begin to compare to the hurts done to us by those we love. There is no pain like betrayal, but only someone we have trusted can betray us.

> For it was not an enemy that reproached me; then I could have borne it. Neither was it he that hated me that did magnify himself against me; then would I have hidden myself from him. But it was thou, a man mine equal, my guide, and my familiar friend. We took sweet counsel together, and walked into the house of God in company.
>
> PSALM 55:12-14

A senior pastor went through a particularly painful church split. The worst part of it, for him, was that his most trusted senior associate had led the rebellion and nearly destroyed the church. "I am like Jacob in Genesis 32:10," he told me sadly.

"How so?" I asked.

"I crossed over with my staff, and now we have become two bands."

I met a man in Dallas, Texas, who had just gone

through a bitter divorce. In the settlement he lost a ranch he had inherited from his father. At that time his ex-wife was living there with her lawyer.

"They're not even bothering to get married," he said. "My two children see her go up to bed every night with that shyster. They're living on a ranch that's been in my family for nearly a hundred years. Now, how do I forgive that?"

START MAKING SENSE!

The mercy we want the most from God and find the most difficult to grant others is forgiveness. If it is true that to err is human and to forgive is divine, then only God can forgive. The problem is, we are commanded to forgive even as we are forgiven. In his Sermon on the Mount, Jesus ties receiving forgiveness to granting it. But there really are some things that seem impossible to forgive.

Forgiveness is mercy in action at life's most painful points. Granting mercy to those who have been merciless to us runs contrary to our every carnal impulse. An eye for an eye makes sense when you are hurting. Turning the other cheek does not! That's the problem with a lot of the things Jesus taught. They don't make sense. Giving away your money doesn't make sense. Losing your life certainly doesn't make sense. And forgiving people that deserve to be hated? Be honest now, doesn't that sound just a bit loony? Unless, of course, we remember that we deserve for God to hate us, and yet he—in his mercy—died in our place.

A PATH FULL OF POTHOLES

Again, the act of forgiving is infinitely more difficult than talking about it. There are two different types of situations in which we must forgive others. The one is far more difficult than the other. But even the "easier" one is fraught with danger.

The first situation is when someone asks for forgiveness. The obvious challenge here is withholding forgiveness. "Have mercy" is another way of saying, "Please forgive me." The person is pleading, "You have the power, and every right, not to forgive me. I would not blame you if you refused, but I beg for mercy." That is a true apology and ought to get forgiveness every time. The fact is, not even such an earnest plea will melt the merciless.

Why not have mercy on such a repentant sinner? The simple answer is revenge—the desire to inflict hurt. The unforgiving think, *If they need my forgiveness, I will withhold it. If mercy is what they long for, they shall have none from me. That will punish them.* Of course it never does. It just punishes the unforgiving. Unforgiveness makes people dark and bitter and full of acid, but it does not punish anyone else. The merciless are among the unhappiest people in all the earth.

Such moments of confusion and repentance hold a hidden danger. When my enemy hurls himself at my feet and pleads for mercy, I may be tempted to withhold mercy. I may also grant it but gloat in the victory. *Ah ha! I won! At long last you see it. I was right and you were wrong, wrong, wrong! I forgive you because now, as then, I am better than you.* Even forgiveness can be extended in regal condescension. *Rise, peasant, your lord and master has forgiven you.*

To forgive the debts of others we must be gracious—releasing them, healing them. We release all hope of being paid what we are owed. If we dare to gloat, we squeeze the juice out. An apology is either an opportunity to release the debt or to get paid at long last.

AM I SUPPOSED TO FORGIVE THAT?

The second circumstance of forgiveness is the sin for which the wrongdoer has not apologized. That is the really hard one for most of us. Someone has hurt us badly, deeply, perhaps even betrayed us, and has never asked forgiveness. Shall we also give them mercy? Jesus says yes, but most of us find it a daunting task.

A man whom I had trusted both personally and professionally betrayed my confidence, then set out to hurt my reputation with mutual friends. I had never felt so much hurt. The shock was stunning. I kept trying to forgive, but months later I still could not seem to find release in the matter. One night I dreamed that my "betrayer" died in a car crash. The image was so vivid and disturbing that upon waking I prayed, "Lord, are you telling me this man is going to die?"

"No," seemed to be the answer in my heart, "I am revealing to you how you really feel. You want him dead. You will not find release until you pray for him to live."

I remember weeping, and praying for him to live, to *really* live in blessedness and prosperity. I prayed for his family, his work and his health. I had never felt so free.

Then some time later I saw him again, and I was shattered at my reaction. I did not want to see him or talk to him or pretend nothing had happened. I felt all the old anger bubbling around inside, and doubt and confusion gripped me. *Had I not forgiven him?* I had felt such liberty. What was the matter with me?

About that time I read a powerful piece by the late Corrie ten Boom. In it she explained that unforgiveness is like ringing a bell. As long as you pull the rope, the bell in the tower rings. Then you make a decision not to ring it anymore. You let go of the rope, and you are free of the unforgiveness. That's fine, but the bell keeps ringing for a while. Your hand is no longer on the rope. You no longer will it to ring, but the momentum of your emotions does not instantly stop because a decision of the will has been made.

In other words, we must make a distinction between our willful unforgiveness and the emotional aftershocks that time and the Spirit can only gradually heal. So we forgive in Jesus' name; we will to forgive and we go on praying blessings instead of curses. But we must remember that in forgiveness, like everything else in the kingdom, we walk by faith, not by feelings. The feelings will come, but for now I must not confuse the emotional impulses of my weak flesh with sinful disobedience.

What we hope for in such matters is closure, and the older I get the less confidence I have in that. In the first place, closure seldom comes. We fantasize the dramatic moment when someone comes to apologize or, at least, to "deal with it." The problem is that after a while we don't even remember what "it" was. Our hurts and wounds get all tangled and confused with too many people and so many complications that sorting it out becomes impossible. Hopes for a real resolution seldom come to pass.

Our best chance is to forgive before we're asked. We must take our hand off the bell rope and let it gradually fade to silence—in *us*. We must remember it has nothing to do with what is going on in anyone else. Have you ever had someone tell you they had forgiven you for an offense you hadn't even realized you had committed? How did you feel? Awkward, I'm sure. What are we supposed to say in such situations?

If we truly want to forgive someone before they ask our forgiveness, we should not tell them so. When or if they ever come to us for forgiveness, we will be able to say with sincerity that it was forgiven long ago. But if we go to them with our "forgiveness," it may sound sanctimonious and pretentious, making them defensive instead of repentant. Forgive in your heart. Perhaps the Holy Spirit will provide an opportunity to tell them you have forgiven them, but force it and you will regret it.

WHEN YOU SEEK MERCY

What about when we are the ones who have sinned? There is even a merciful way to seek mercy. A mixed apology is no apology at all. "Please forgive me; I know what I did was not right, but ..." But *nothing!* The only apology that works is absolute. "I was wrong. Please forgive me."

Nothing less.

Nothing more.

Nothing else.

An apology alloyed with even a hint of accusation will fail utterly because it is insincere and self-serving.

Even then we may not be finished. Restitution is the merciful act of the truly repentant. If I have stolen money from you and ask forgiveness without repayment, I am merciless indeed. I have your money. Now I want your forgiveness, and I offer nothing in return except an apology. What is *that?*

A man was once called a liar in a public meeting. Later his accuser wrote him an impassioned letter, confessing that she was wrong. She said, "I now see you were telling the truth, and I ask you to forgive me."

He wrote her back that he certainly did forgive her, but he also told her that public accusations and private apologies do not equate. He urged her for her own spiritual well-being to contact as many in that meeting as possible and clear the matter with them. When restitution can be made, it needs to be made.

In Acts 16, Paul and Silas were unjustly beaten and imprisoned at Philippi in northern Greece. Later, when the local magistrates discovered that Paul was a Roman citizen, they sent a couple of sergeants to release them and begged them to "go in peace." On the surface this seems reasonable, perhaps, and we may imagine Paul granting forgiveness and meekly leaving town. That would be the Christian thing to do. Right? Wrong.

Paul said, "You beat me publicly and defame the gospel I preach in front of the whole town, then you apologize privately. Not in this life! Come down here yourselves and lead me out in front of everyone and let your apology be as public as your sin" (Acts 16:37, author's paraphrase).

That's rough mercy, perhaps, but it is *real* mercy. It is not sentimental, pretend, play-nice-and-don't-ruffle-any-feathers mercy. It is real Christian, let-me-show-you-how-to-really-clear-this-up mercy. In the final analysis, that is the only kind of forgiveness that works. The yes-I-forgive-you-and-I'll-quietly-leave-like-nothing-ever-happened kind is a patronizing pat on the head, if not out-and-out hypocrisy.

TO FORGIVE IS DIVINE

So what about the man who lost his ranch and his wife and his kids to a Fort Worth lawyer? How does he forgive that? If forgiveness is divine, then he must let the power of the Divine flow through him. Who could drive past the gate of his great-grandfather's ranch and know that his wife is in there sleeping with the lawyer who gutted him in court? Who could forgive *that?* Who, indeed? The One who forgave his murderers, prayed for his mockers, died for his false friends and redeemed his own rebellious creation. Whatever you need to forgive, the thing is to let the Lord do it through you.

At a certain church in the Southwest, a huge man came forward for prayer after I spoke on forgiveness. I have never seen a man in such spiritual turmoil. His huge frame was racked with sobs as he told me an unforgettable story.

He was a deputy sheriff. Answering a call one night, he found there had been a shotgun murder in a local bar. He arrested the killer without resistance. The man just handed over the weapon and held out his hands for the cuffs.

The female victim on the floor was clearly dead. A shotgun at close range can just about cut a body in half. When they turned the corpse over, it was the deputy's daughter. The horror of what he saw on that barroom floor quickly turned to blind rage. It would have been easy for him to kill his daughter's murderer. He had twenty-four-hour-a-day access to the man's cell. He told me he had wanted to kill him, had ached to. He told me he had fantasized it, imagined it, plotted it, but had never gone through with it.

"It's not so much that I want to forgive," he sobbed. "I *have* to. I must! It's killing me. Help me. Please, God, help me!"

Another man from the congregation knelt beside him. We pretended that he was the murderer. "Have mercy on me," the murderer pleaded. "Please forgive me."

"Christ in you, the hope of glory," I whispered in the deputy's ears. "Let Christ do it. His hands in yours. His mind, his will, *his* mercy."

I will never, ever forget those huge hands trembling so pitifully as they reached out to rest on the "killer's" head. Nor will I forget the gut-wrenching sound of that tough policeman's voice as mercy flowed out from Christ within him.

"I forgive you," he wailed. "I do. I do. I do. I really forgive you."

At that moment God filled him with the Holy Spirit. Release and joy came in a wild rush of tears and laughter. The next day he and his wife drove down to the state pen to tell the real killer.

How can you forgive your ex and her lawyer? Like that.

Benny Gambino

Benny Gambino looked down at the slowly hardening cement around his feet and he knew he was going to die. He tugged at the ropes involuntarily, but he knew it was futile. "Fast Willie" Rizzo and Fat Grego Martini were professionals, not the kind of lightweights to make that kind of mistake.

Rizzo laughed when he saw Benny's pathetic struggles. He had a kind of high-pitched, girlish laugh that sent a shiver of despair down Benny's spine. It seemed strange to Benny that the most feared hit man in Chicago should have such a laugh.

Rizzo was a wiry man with a thin, sharp face and beady malevolent eyes that oozed mockery. The word was that he could kill a man in a hundred ways. To use such a crazy old thing as this cement boot was the mob's way of saying to Gambino, Look, you broke a tradition, you die in a traditional way.

"Hey, look," Rizzo piped, "our boy here thinks he can break the ropes. Ain't that true, Benny? You think you can break the ropes? Can you do that?"

"Huh, yeah," Martini said in his dull-witted raspy

voice. He was a great, fat hulk of a man with blank eyes and a brutish face. "Well, even if he does, he ain't goin' nowhere but to da bottom of da lake. Huh, huh."

Benny's heart sank. No appeal was possible, and no rescue was coming. These two, this thin little creep and his half-witted ox of a partner, were going to take the boat out to the middle of the lake and just drop him in the water. Just like that. Down, down into the pitch-black iciness of the lake to drown with his feet in a tub of cement. He hated the thought that the last sound he would ever hear was Martini's stupid voice and Rizzo's girlish giggle.

"Hey, I think Carlo is comin'," said Rizzo.

"Huh, huh," laughed Martini the ox. "I guess he's coming to tell youse good-bye. Huh, huh, huh."

The door to the cabin cruiser opened and Carlo Infanti himself stepped in. This was *cappo di cappi*, boss of bosses. Infanti—or Carlo the Babe, as he was known but never called to his face—was perhaps not as powerful as the five New York families, but he was certainly the most powerful man in the Midwestern Mafia.

Rizzo and the ox stood up to show their respect, but they said nothing. Nobody said much when Infanti was in a room.

"Is it ready?" Infanti asked, but his eyes were on Benny, not the two killers.

"Yeah," said Rizzo. "The cement ain't quite set

up yet. By the time we get out to the middle it'll be hard enough. He ain't goin' nowhere, Mr. Infanti."

"Huh, huh," laughed Martini, "'cept down, that is. Huh, huh."

"Shut up," said Infanti, still keeping his eyes on Benny. "Now look, you. I had hopes for you. You think I wanted this, Benny? You're wrong. I had plans for you. Big plans. You got brains. For a lousy few thousand bucks, now you got yourself a chance to be fish food."

"I'm sorry, Mr. Infanti," pleaded Benny. "Please, you gotta believe me."

A strange smile played across Infanti's face as he said, "You know, Benny, I do believe you."

"You do?"

"Yeah, I do. I knew you was too smart to steal from *me*, but I hadda teach you a lesson. I hadda know that you'll never do that again. Never borrow like that. You understand me?"

Benny tried to comprehend. What was Infanti saying? He couldn't mean …

"Hey," shouted Rizzo. "Answer Mr. Infanti! He's talkin' to you. Ain't you got no respect?"

"It's all right, Rizzo," Infanti said softly. "You boys get him outta there before we have to use a jackhammer."

Benny Gambino could not believe his good fortune. As the two hit men cut the ropes and helped him step out of the goop in the tub, Gambino virtually sobbed his thanks to Infanti over and over. Finally he fell, still dripping globs of cement, at

Infanti's feet. In a gesture even older than the Mafia, Benny Gambino kissed Mr. Infanti's hand and pledged eternal loyalty.

Some months later it was reported to Infanti that Gambino had crippled a certain two-bit gambler over an unpaid debt. This was well within Gambino's right as far as that went. The loan-sharking in that neighborhood was Gambino's business. And it also made a nice profit for Infanti.

But what Gambino forgot was that this particular gambler was married to Carlo Infanti's niece. Gambino knew this, but his rage at being stiffed on the five hundred dollars was uncontrollable. He sent two thugs from the lower East Side out to the gambler's house and they used tire irons to pulverize the man's kneecaps. The gambler's name was Johnny Tricotti. People called him Johnny Treetop because he was tall and thin.

"Hey, Rizzo," Infanti said when he heard about Johnny Tricotti. "When Gambino stole dat money from me, did I knock his kneecaps off?"

"No, Mr. Infanti, you didn't do that."

"No!" Infanti shouted, hammering the desk with his huge fist. "I pulled that slob outta the cement. Well, that was my mistake! But mistakes can be fixed. Go down there, Rizzo. Take Fat Grego with you and finish the job. Do it now. Right now!"

By this time Infanti was almost screaming. Rizzo had never seen the boss this angry, and he did not want to make a mistake.

"You want that we should sink him in da lake, Mr. Infanti?" he asked.

"No," Infanti said, calming himself and straightening his tie. "No. Just walk in an' say, Mr. Infanti said that he let *you* go, and you shoulda let the husband of his niece off the hook. Tell 'im this is for Johnny Treetop. Then just whack him. Don't make no big deal out of it."

* * *

When the Master finished telling this story, his friends were silent. They did not know what to make of it. This grim little story about the Mafia confused them.

"But look," Peter protested. "Mercy is all well and good, but aren't there any lines? I mean, doesn't it come to an end someplace?"

"Does it?" the Master asked.

"Well, sure," Peter went on. "I'm not talking about this Mafia stuff. But surely at some point you have to say, 'Show me the money.' Everybody has his limits. Right?"

"God has no limits," the Master said. "He had mercy on you and he expects you to have mercy on one another. Whack and ye shall be whacked. Have mercy and you get mercy. Is that too hard to understand?"

"No," his friends said, but really they thought it was (see Matthew 18:23-35).

Part Three

Mercy Most Needed:
Toward an Activist Church
in a Waiting World

*"He that despiseth his neighbor sinneth;
but he that hath mercy on the poor, happy is he."*

PROVERBS 14:21

Twelve

Mercy and Zeal in the Church

Humor is where you find it, and I have always thought the team name for Wake Forest University's sports program is an absolute riot. The Demon Deacons! You gotta love it. It reminds me of my early days refereeing in the Washington, D.C. area. The sports headlines generated by the parochial schools were a scream.

Blessed Virgin Stomps St. Pius X
or
Bishop Gonzaga Ends Dream
for Immaculate Conception

But I suppose my all-time favorite is this one, from the South.

Demon Deacons Prepare for
Physical Test at Citadel

Most football teams want their teams named for fearsome beasts of prey. Eagles, Bears, Tigers and ... Demon Deacons? When you think of it that way, lions and hawks don't look very scary. But a demonic church leader? *That* is to be feared!

The headline was pithy in another way, too. It is when they struggle in the physical dimension that deacons can get the most demonized. One bizarre story on the various wire services told of a woman who lost it at choir practice at a Baptist church. She turned and threw acid in the face of the woman behind her.

What happens? How do we get from singing "Gentle Jesus Meek and Mild" to baptizing each other with acid? The problem is not so much that we are capable of doing evil and violent things in the sanctuary but that we can do them and feel righteous about it. A dear friend told me that in one church he pastored, "they" blew up his car.

"Who is *they?*" I asked him. "Drug dealers and porno kings?"

"No," he answered. "It was church folks."

They ran a fuse right into the gas tank of his car and blew it to smithereens!

We want to think that if we differ ideologically with some homicidal maniac, we are different ethically. By some twisted logic, Timothy McVeigh was certain that what he was doing was moral. He did not become the worst mass murderer in American history because he longed to commit a heinous act. He did it because, like all terrorists, he believed that his "cause," whatever it might have been, was more important than the sanctity of the lives he buried under the rubble of the Federal Building.

That is what makes a zealot.

THE MORALITY OF MERCY

Zealots are not dangerous because they have no morals, they are dangerous because they have perverted their morals. The demon deacon who dropped dynamite down my friend's gas tank was certain he and his cause were more moral than the pastor and his family asleep in the parsonage. There is nothing more dangerous in all the world than a religious zealot who feels justified by his cause.

That cause—the ideal or conviction or teaching—that justifies the zealot's actions also robs him of all mercy. Mercy is excess baggage to the true zealot. Indeed, in the scheme of the zealot's life, mercy is actually counterproductive and feels like compromise, which is the most immoral vice in his universe.

The Pharisees were outraged at Jesus' watered-down approach to adultery. In fact, the woman they hurled at his feet was not their concern. They were not nearly so intent on exposing her as they were on exposing Jesus. They wanted everyone to see that he was soft on adultery, that he lacked a fierce commitment to the immutability of the law. The life of one adulteress was hardly of significance to a howling pack of merciless legalists. She was merely a convenient victim test to smoke out the squeamish—especially Jesus.

Their agenda was the reinforcement of the law. Total dedication to the law, no matter how much blood was spilled, was their minimum daily adult requirement. To think of the woman's shame, her fear, her need for hope was unthinkable. That's just the kind of thing they figured Jesus was thinking, and they knew exactly how to make that weakness clear to everyone.

I once preached a funeral in a small church. A cold January rain pelted the knot of sodden mourners clustered around the graveside. The local pastor was an elderly man whose own wife was at the parsonage in the last stages of cancer. Having forgotten his own slicker, he rummaged under the front seat until he came up with his wife's orange raincoat. It was a bit on the frilly side, but the necessity of his not getting sick seemed more important in the moment than wearing appropriate raingear.

"I think everyone will understand if I wear this," he said to me as we slogged out to the tiny green funeral tent. "I just cannot get sick with my wife so ill. I'm sure they'll understand."

He was wrong. The howls of complaint thawed out the phone lines even before the pound cake was gone at the covered-dish supper back in the cozy church hall. The discouraged old man accepted the fury of the church mothers in mute acquiescence. Like the victim of any stoning, he knew that appeals for mercy were useless. This was not about mercy. This was about community pride. There were visitors there, after all, who had seen the pastor do a graveside service in a woman's raincoat. What would they think? The law of appearances had been broken! Somebody had to die, and the likeliest candidate was their own pastor, preoccupied with a dying wife.

Mercy would have understood, made allowances and granted latitude. Mercy would have seen past the readily visible and discerned the greater need. Zealots stood in the cold winter rain, heaping praise on the dead and derision on the living. Mercy would have zipped the grave up quickly and bustled an old pastor inside for a steaming cup of tea and some dry clothes. Mercy might at least have stripped off its own lined overcoat and worn the woman's orange raincoat.

The mercilessness of a "Christianity" that replaces the Spirit of Christ with an agenda is remorseless and unrelenting. I am a conservative, antiabortion Republican, but I am grieved at the shrill, merciless insolence of some of us. We do not have God's permission to demean and debase. We do not have God's permission to expand the level of our own rhetoric until it inflames the murderous and maniacal, then wash our hands like Pilate. And we do not have God's permission to put mercy to death on the altar of conservative (or liberal) political correctness.

What bitter irony that for much of the two-thousand-year history of Christ's church, his teachings on mercy have been crucified by a cultural religion hell-bent on fulfilling its own agenda with the weapons of the world. From the ancient Crusades to the present-day war in Ireland and abortion clinic bombings, we seem perfectly willing to blithely lay aside the call to be merciful by a Christ whose mercies we claim for ourselves.

For all our spiritual talk, the American church has lost a real and precious mercy that must be regained. The Western church is angry. It rumbles ominously, warning that eruptions can come at any moment. Instead of being the antidote for our society's ruthlessness and remorselessness, the church frequently reflects it.

MERCY AND CULTURE

The power of mercy to change culture and change lives is at the epicenter of the true Christian movement. But compared to the sexiness of the sword, mercy makes slow and delicate progress. For nearly four hundred years, Christians died for their faith. Then Rome's pagan emperor horribly misread what was apparently a genuine vision from God, and Christians began killing for their faith. Killing for one's faith is vastly different from dying for it.

The teachings of Jesus were all right for women such as his wife and mother, but not for a warrior prince like the Roman Emperor Constantine. On the eve of a crucial battle, Constantine saw a cross in the sky and heard God's voice saying, "In this sign conquer." He commanded that crosses be painted on all the shields in the Roman army, and sure enough the next day's battle was a glorious victory.

It did not, evidently, occur to Constantine that by embracing the Cross, the spirit of the world can be conquered. In the Garden of Gethsemane Jesus did not paint a cross on his shield or rally the troops for an assault on Pilate's garrison in the Antonia Fortress. He died at Gethsemane before he ever reached Calvary. He let go of self-will and the power of the sword and submitted himself to the eternal purpose of God. His was the greatest act of mercy in history. He died for Constantine and for murderers and their victims, and for abortion doctors and the babies they kill, and for homosexuals and those who despise them.

Is there some inherent thread of violence in biblical Christianity? No! There is a sword in the hand of Islam as there was in the hand of its founder. It is in Islam that we find the concept of *jihad,* or holy war. It is not inconsistent with Islam that *mujahadin* (holy warriors) do slaughter in Allah's name. Certainly there have been "Christian" wars and warriors, but they are a perversion of what Christ taught. There is no philosophical or theological seed anywhere in biblical Christianity that can produce a terrorist without mercy. There is no office in the New Testament Church called *mujahadin.*

Jesus was a merciful man who wrought a merciful work for the salvation of the world so that we might be merciful to one another. When we forget what was done unto and by him, we lose the mercy which makes us like him and not like the beasts of prey.

In Judges 12, a bitter civil strife among the Hebrew tribes turned to savage and remorseless warfare. At the fords of the Jordan, the army of Gilead intercepted the defeated and desperately fleeing soldiers from Ephraim. These pathetic Ephraimite refugees hoped to escape by claiming to be from Gilead themselves. The soldiers of Gilead were not so easily fooled. They knew that a peculiar speech pattern of the Ephraimite accent made it impossible for them to begin words with a "sh" sound.

"Say Shibboleth," they would demand.

If it sounded like Sibboleth, the wretched man died instantly. "There fell at that time of the Ephraimites forty and two thousand" (Judges 12:6).

We must cease the slaughter at the fords of the Jordan and lay aside all the shibboleths by which we demonize and make enemies of our brothers and sisters.

Just before his death, Jamie Buckingham said to me, "I am convinced that in most matters it is far more important to be kind than right."

I suspect that our merciful God would agree.

The Knight

The crusader was in a fury as he charged up the staircase. His friend, a handsome youth named Klaus, lay dead behind him with an arrow through his heart. They had been born in the same Black Forest village, had kept vigil on the same night and had been knighted together the next day in a unique joint ceremony. Now Klaus would never again see his mother in Germany. Friedrich, as the crusader was called, knew that it would fall to him to bear the bad news home to a small town on the edge of the Schwarzwald.

Nothing had gone right on this entire Crusade. They had sat in Sicily for three months, growing restless, fighting among themselves and waiting for their emperor and the absurd French king, whom they detested, to decide issues of logistics and protocol. Their fervor to liberate the holy city of Jerusalem from the hands of the infidel waned, then wasted itself in debauchery. Friedrich and Klaus found

Sicilian wine and women to their liking, but what they wanted was war. They temporarily drained off pent-up energy in the brothels and taverns of the island, but it did not satisfy. Blood—Islamic blood, Arab blood—was the libation they longed for.

Finally they had taken ship with great fanfare, their armor gleaming in the Mediterranean sun. At last! The great Crusade to free Jerusalem was afloat. The sea voyage had been a nightmare of sickness and bad food. Their royal overlords had cut expenses by buying cheap supplies and hiring less than regal transport. One of the ships even sank, meaning the loss of many knights, but none of them had been German, so the two young crusaders had not grieved too much.

Then on the first day of marching inland, their own commander's horse had bolted into a river, promptly drowning the great knight. A week later some kind of exotic fever hit the crusader camp, and knights fell like flies. None of the sturdy Germans were in the least surprised when the French furled their flags and left the field. The Teutonic warriors heaped derision upon the Franks as they headed back to their ships. But when the French were gone, gloom settled in upon them. Their forces were too small and weakened by sickness to even reach Jerusalem, let alone take it. Deserted by their hated allies, the Germans were filled with confusion and frustration.

Finally their officers determined they would not go home empty-handed. Wheeling the small army of knights to the north, they attacked a peaceful Turkish city without warning. Surely many Moslems were there. Why go all the way to the Holy Land when there was a city to be looted so close at hand?

The resistance was light and futile. The knights were heavily armored machines riding over the pathetic defenses like the wrath of God they knew themselves to be. The army's bloodlust was insatiable. The desperate screams of ravished women pierced the night. Friedrich saw small children trampled under the hooves of the relentless German chargers. What did it matter? These infidels should pay the terrible price for the crusaders' suffering, their commander's death and the French defection. Let the infidels' women scream, their babies perish and the men fall under the crusader lances. This was holy work, not massacre. Let God be glorified!

Then the fatal arrow somehow, from somewhere, found a chink in Klaus' chain mail. It should never have happened. The fighting was over. Loot was being carried out of burning houses. Who was left to shoot the arrow? Friedrich searched the windows for the archer. Where was he?

A movement, just there to his left, caught Friedrich's attention. A narrow staircase led to an upstairs dwelling. Someone was there. Was it the killer of his boyhood friend? Friedrich was not of a mind to care about such details. Some life must be forfeited for that of his friend.

Screaming as he came, the knight charged up the stairs with his sword drawn. The fragile door gave way to one ferocious kick, and the crusader plunged across the threshold ready for the enemy within. His practiced military eye surveyed the scene. Somehow this tranquil room had miraculously escaped the carnage in the streets below.

A solitary old man knelt in the center of the room with his arms around a small girl. Fear filled his eyes, and the child screamed, twisting her tiny hand in the old man's beard. She hid her face in her grandfather's shoulder and sobbed at the gruesome sight of this ferocious intruder. The arms and tunic of the massive soldier looming above them were drenched in blood. The warrior's face was contorted in rage, and a broadsword that was longer than the girl herself gleamed ominously above their heads.

"German?" her grandfather asked hopefully. It was a language he had learned only a smattering of for trade purposes. "Du bist ein Deutschlander?"

"Ja," snarled the knight, and kicked the door shut behind him.

"Have mercy," pleaded the old man. "Please have mercy on us!"

At this the crusader roared in laughter. Did this old infidel think he was a woman? He did not leave his home and fatherland and join the Crusades to have mercy.

The sword slashed like angry lightning, and the

old man's corpse fell at his granddaughter's feet. Her horror stifled her scream. She looked up from the nightmare of her grandfather's remains to stare again at the murderer in her house. Who was this monster? She studied the simple design upon his tunic. Where had she seen it before? She did not know what it could mean. A plain white cross on a deep blue field. It was the last thing she saw.

Thirteen

Mercy and the Compassionate Church

As an undergraduate student at the University of Maryland, I needed an easy two-credit 'A' to boost my grade-point average and fill an elective requirement. I took a course in canoeing and enjoyed it very much. In fact, I still canoe occasionally. One coed, however, saw things differently.

After two days of classroom preparation our instructor announced that "today we will finally get out on the water."

"What do you mean?" the coed wailed.

"Well, isn't this what you have been waiting for?" he asked her. "Aren't you ready to get out on the lake and actually do it yourself?"

I shall never forget the look of abject horror on that girl's face as she cried out, "No! I can't swim. I hate boats. I hate water. And you can't make me do it!"

"But ..." he protested.

"But nothing!" she said, gathering up her books. "I'm going right now to drop this course."

"Fine," agreed the amazed instructor. "But why did you sign up for it?"

"I thought it was a theory course," she announced. "I took music theory and made an 'A,' but I did not have to learn to play Chopin."

Some things defy much theorizing. At some point, poems about baseball run dry, and the diamond begs for somebody to actually throw the ball. How long can a course on the "Theory of the Native American Canoe" last until a paddle is actually dipped into a cool, bright stream somewhere?

A CALL TO GET DOWN AND DIRTY

Mercy has a similar problem. Theorizing about mercy is easy. It's *showing* mercy that we hate. Some of us don't even like to be reminded that we are to show mercy. The story of the Good Samaritan, for example, has become little more than a biblical Aesop's fable. It makes a nice illustration for moralistic children's sermons, but once trivialized it loses the devastating punch Jesus intended for it to have. The story was not meant to be anecdotal material for Sunday school quarterlies, calling upon children not to push in the lunch line. It is a kick straight to the solar plexus of Christian theory courses. It is a call to lay aside our religious robes and legal rhetoric and to get down and dirty.

Compassion is something we feel. Mercy must be *shown*. Mercy is only real when it is demonstrated. Heartrending pictures of dying African babies tear at our emotions, but until feelings become flesh and deed they cannot be called mercy. I once heard a woman explain that she could not bear to volunteer at the homeless shelter because her spiritual gift was mercy, and such human tragedy depressed her. She had confused *mercy* with *sensitivity*. By being unable to deal with her emotions, she became unable to show mercy to the hurting. By this formula only the hard-hearted can be merciful.

The whole of Christ's teaching on mercy is this: God saw us in the tragedy of our lostness, and out of his compassion he acted in sacrificial mercy to save us. Now he expects us not only to feel what he feels but to turn those feelings into sacrificial deeds. To see, to feel, to hurt with the hurting is useless if you stand apart with your arms crossed. This is the theme of the Good Samaritan story. Jesus does not tell us what the priest and the Levite felt at the sight of the pitiful, wounded victim. What might they have felt? Fear, maybe. The self-preservation impulse often puts mercy to death: *Stay clear of this. Do not get involved.* Or maybe it was disgust. It is no sin to feel repulsion at the bloody victims of this world. Their open wounds are disgusting. What about compassion? Did the two religious men feel no compassion? We do not know, because Jesus gave us no insight whatsoever into their feelings. We only know that regardless of what they felt, they *did* nothing.

Is there, then, no connection between compassion and mercy? Certainly there is. In fact, Jesus said the Samaritan "had compassion on him" the moment he saw the poor fellow who had been so brutally robbed. But it did not end there. "[He] went to him, and bound up his wounds, pouring in oil and wine, and set him on his own beast, and brought him to an inn, and took care of him. And on the morrow, when he departed, he took out two pence, and gave them to the host, and said unto him, Take care of him; and whatever thou spendest more, when I come again, I will repay thee" (Luke 10:34-35).

His compassion grew feet and walked at considerable expense, personal involvement and physical risk. Perhaps the brigands were still about, waiting to set upon anyone who came to help.

A NECESSARY JOB...
FOR SOMEONE ELSE

Most would agree that mercy is a good thing, especially if they are on the receiving end. Just don't expect them to pay for it. The mercy of many, even those whose hearts bleed the most profusely, ends at the edge of the road. Actually climbing down to the bleeding person lying naked in the ditch is unthinkable to many. We want to think about the needs of the world, pray about them, weep about them, grieve over them, even be outraged by them, but we don't want to meet those needs ourselves, much less get the blood and mud on our hands.

It is apparent from Jesus' Good Samaritan story that he viewed mercy as being apart from the ostentation of religious observance, and independent of national and cultural frontiers. Equally apparent is the premium the Master placed on mercy. Mercy seems to be more important to God than positions of leadership, of greater value than public piety and more precious than doctrinal correctness. The Samaritan was, after all, still a Samaritan. He was of a mixed race so confused in their worship practices that they saw Mt. Gerazim as being of greater significance than the temple in Jerusalem. Jesus did not call upon his fellow Jews to become Samaritans. He was not asking them to change their doctrine but their deeds.

"Which, now, of these three, thinkest thou, was neighbor unto him that fell among the thieves?"

"He that showed mercy," one listener answered.

"Then said Jesus unto him, 'Go, and *do* thou likewise.'"

Jesus was concerned with mercy in action. "Go, and *do* mercy," he commanded (Luke 10:37).

A SHOCK TO OUR PAROCHIALISM

The shocker in Jesus' original version of the Good Samaritan is the casting of roles. The religious types among his own Jewish people are shown as heartless and without mercy. Instead he chose a despicable Samaritan to play the good guy.

I have a friend who is a modern Israeli living in Jerusalem. He says that to understand the effect of this in Jesus' day, we must imagine the story being told today with a Palestinian as the hero! Maybe it might sound like this.

An Israeli soldier serving in the West Bank was wounded in an ambush near Hebron. An orthodox rabbi passed by and saw the soldier lying beside the road. The rabbi could not tell from the car window whether the soldier was dead or alive. If he touched a dead body the rabbi would be unclean, and it was the day before Passover. The young soldier looked dead or nearly dead. Anyway, the law is bigger and more important than one life. If the soldier were an orthodox Jew, he would not be in uniform anyway. The rabbi drove on. He wanted to be in Jerusalem well before sundown.

Then a liberal professor at Hebrew University passed by. He also peered at the wounded soldier. *What was this boy doing out here anyway?* the professor asked himself. The professor did not approve of the Israeli handling of the West Bank. Of course he felt badly for the soldier. But he also understood the rage of the oppressed. Who had compassion on the Arabs? *Not many of my fellow Israelis,* he thought. Well, he did. He drove on, visualizing peace and cooperation.

Just then a Palestinian from Jericho came along. He was a wealthy man who owned two restaurants and three gift shops. He braked his Mercedes to an abrupt stop and leapt out, dragging the wounded Israeli into the back seat. He could tell the boy was barely alive and needed help immediately. The Palestinian drove furiously toward the nearby Israeli army checkpoint. If he could just get the boy there they would radio for a helicopter. It did occur to him that he was taking a risk to drive into an Israeli checkpoint with a bloody soldier in his back seat. Then he thought of his own son about the same age who was studying at a university in the United States. The Palestinian merchant floored the Benz and prayed he would get there in time.

Imagine Jesus telling that story in Jerusalem today! It's amazing that he stayed alive as long as he did. It is a great story, but why would he put it in such a shocking way?

It was an obvious effort to blast his hearers out of their smug, self-serving parochialism and into a life of merciful service to humanity. Basically the questions is, "Can you do mercy as well as a Samaritan?"

God knows that sometimes we must be shocked into action. Suppose Jesus should appear in an American church and say, "There is a Communist Chinese doctor who treats the poor for free. Do you call that mercy?"

"Yes, Lord, we do."

"So do I," he might say. "Can you do as well as a Chinese Communist?"

The story of the Good Samaritan is not mere messianic theologizing. It is a summons to action. Jesus obviously envisioned a church that *did* mercy, not one that talked about it and never moved. The forgotten poor, the hurting, the doomed and the damned are not waiting for the church to understand mercy. They are just waiting for whoever gets there first to show a little practical kindness. Jesus seemed to think that ought to be the church.

The Goofy Judge

"I sentence you," shouted the judge, "to watch seventy-five hours of Monty Python and Mr. Bean, with no less than four junior-high school boys."

"But, your honor," protested the silver-haired defendant, "what kind of a ..."

"Ninety hours!" said the judge.

"You're crazy ..." the defendant began wailing.

"One hundred hours!" boomed the judge and pounded his gavel.

"Look, your honor, you can't sentence me to ..."

"PLUS!" shouted the judge, thundering down his massive gavel, "Plus you must buy them all popcorn and sodas, and eat some yourself. I warn you, if you say one more word, I will find you in contempt of court and that, Mr. Bromley, would mean being ordered to do Charlie Chaplin imitations down at the Woodrow Wilson Junior High. Do you understand?"

"Yes, your honor," Bromley responded dejectedly, his beefy shoulders slumping.

"Don't be so downcast, Bromley," said the judge tenderly. "You might enjoy this. In fact, I sentence you to enjoy it."

"But your honor ..."

"Ah, ah, ah— tut, tut, Bromley," scolded his honor.

"Yes, your honor. But your honor," protested the elderly man. "My shirt is dirty and smelly. I cannot entertain kids like this."

"That's what I was waiting for you to say!" shouted the judge. "Bailiff, get a Michael Jordan jersey for Bromley here. The kids will love that!"

"Thank you, sir," Bromley said.

"Bailiff," the judge said firmly, "next case."

Two young law clerks stood in the back of the courtroom, watching the proceedings. One was an attractive woman in a smart wool suit. Obviously astonished at the recent sentencing, she turned her gaze on the other, an unkempt youth in a rumpled jacket. He was clearly less prosperous than his female colleague.

"You work for this guy?" she asked.

"Yeah," he said with a shrug. "Different, huh."

"Different?" she snorted. "Try weird."

"You haven't seen anything."

"Hey, what did that guy Bromley do anyway?" she asked.

"He was mean to the kids in his neighborhood. Always yelling at 'em, cussin' at 'em, stuff like that."

"Well, what about this next case?" she pressed, already intrigued. "What did this guy do?"

"Fell in a cesspool," explained the disheveled clerk of the court. In a few seconds that fact was obvious to the entire courtroom.

"Oh, my goodness!" gasped the young woman as she held a hanky to her face. "That smell is nauseating."

The defendant was in fact still coated in the sickening green proof of his plunge into the sewage pit. He was a young man, but it was difficult to tell much else because of the condition he was in. He stood alone, head down before the judge. Even the bailiffs kept their distance.

"Guilty, I assume," said the judge.

"Yes, your honor," muttered the slime-encrusted boy.

"Ready for sentencing?" asked the judge.

"Yes, your honor."

"I sentence you to be cleaned up," announced the judge, rapping the gavel sharply.

"What … ?" exclaimed the female clerk, dropping the hanky from her face for a split second.

"AND …" shouted the judge, to still the instant commotion in the courtroom, "and to spend two hours a week in the local nursing home. The first hour you will wash bedpans. The second hour you will blow up balloons in the Alzheimer's unit. If you do not leave the place cleaner and happier than when you arrived, I will summon you again."

"Thank you, your honor," whispered the miserable defendant. "That is very fair."

"Fair!" snorted the female clerk. "That's not fair! That's goofy!"

"But, your honor," wailed the boy coated in filth. "Who will clean me up? No one will even touch me. You sentenced me to be cleaned up, but who will do it?"

"I will!" shouted the judge with what appeared to be a note of joy in his voice.

With that he donned a beanie topped with a musical propeller and leapt to his feet. The smiling judge gave the propeller a spin and it began to play *Pop Goes the Weasel* at an impossible volume. "This should be fun!" crowed the judge. "Man, do you stink. Ha, ha! Oh, yes! This will be great. And that young lady back there, yes *you*,

you are sentenced to help me."

Realizing that the judge was pointing at her, the female clerk cried out spontaneously, "You must be crazy!"

"Duh!" said the judge. "Of course I'm crazy. Now here's your beanie. Come on, wake up. This will be great fun! Great fun! Wake up! Put on your beanie. Wake up!"

* * *

"Wake up, Judge Mahoney," pleaded the voice. "Please wake up."

Judge Margaret Mahoney sat up on the couch in her office, staring uncomprehendingly at her law clerk. Relief rushed through her. A dream. Only a dream.

"Oh, Laura," said the judge, "thanks for awakening me. I was dreaming."

"You scared me, your honor," said the young clerk, helping to steady the older woman as she struggled to rise and get her feet back in the plain black pumps she had kicked off at the end of the sofa. "I was shaking you and yelling. You were really out."

"Sorry," said the judge. "What time is it?"

"Nearly three o'clock. Time for you to pass sentence on the Watkins kid. Are you ready? The principals are all in the court."

"Yes, and please bring me my beanie," said the judge, straightening her hair.

"Beanie?" Laura asked.

"Did I say beanie? Not beanie ... robe. Please bring me my robe."

"You know," Laura said, helping the judge shrug into the black robe, "I really despise this Watkins boy. He is just the nastiest kid."

"Nasty?" asked the judge.

"Well, you know," Laura answered. "It's just an expression. Anyway, what were you dreaming?"

"I was dreaming of myself when I was young," said the graying judge, pausing with her hand on the doorknob. "I was about your age. Now buzz the bailiff. I'm ready to come out."

"Yes, your honor," Laura said, reaching for the phone. "Are you gonna throw the book at the Watkins kid?"

"I don't think so, Laura," Judge Mahoney answered. "You remember this. Justice is more complicated than I thought it was at your age. Watkins probably just needs a bath and a grandmother."

"Well, that would be a pretty goofy sentence."

"Wouldn't it just," Judge Mahoney laughed. "Wouldn't it just."

Fourteen

Mercy and the Church in Action

The night before the Alamo fell to the hordes of Santa Ana, the Mexican buglers played the dreaded melody "Degüello." This grim serenade was Santa Ana's musical way of announcing "no quarter." In other words, tomorrow everyone dies. The Texans inside the old chapel-fortress certainly knew the meaning of the beautiful but haunting melody. There was no hope for mercy from Santa Ana.

If the dictator's troops had wanted some kind of musical retort to be hurled back at them, they were disappointed. Colonel Travis' ragtag company of volunteers knew there was not withstanding Santa Ana and his vast army. Not a soul inside the Alamo had the faintest hope of defeating the Mexicans, or of exacting mercy from them.

Mercy is always in the hands of those who have the power to withhold it.

MERCY AND POWER

God has the authority to extend mercy to a repentant, adulterous wife, and he does. God's message to her is, "I love you and I forgive you." It is not, "Have mercy on your husband." But the word of heaven to the husband is exactly that. "Have mercy on your wife." Why? Because the husband has all the cards in his hands. The wife has no trumps and no aces.

Oh, sure, he can claim his rights. Her humble, broken appeal for forgiveness and restoration may be met with a cold rebuff and divorce papers. He can do that. He even has the right to. No one would blame him if he did.

But what does Scripture say?

> Let this mind be in you, which was also in Christ Jesus, who, being in the form of God, thought it not robbery to be equal with God, but made himself of no reputation, and took upon him the form of a servant, and was made in the likeness of men; and, being found in fashion as a man, he humbled himself and became obedient unto death, even the death of the cross.
>
> PHILIPPIANS 2:5-8

The mind of mercy is an issue that must make its appeal not to the weak but to the powerful. The one with the gun is called upon for mercy. In other words, those with the greatest authority and power have the highest opportunity to show mercy.

The property of mercy changes hands faster and more often than Reading Railroad in Monopoly, but it always lies with the powerful. A disobedient and rebellious slave appeals *to his master* for mercy. That night, still smarting from his beating, the slave rises in his hovel, and with ax in hand, steals to his master's bedside. Mercy is now the property of the slave, not the powerless sleeping owner.

When I was at the University of Maryland, a friend of mine joined a campus club just for blacks. I reacted negatively to this because it seemed unfair.

"What if I joined a club just for whites, Charlie?" I pouted. "How would that make you feel?"

"That would be different," Charlie protested.

"Why? What's good for the goose is good for the gander."

"No," Charlie said, "that's not true. It's different, Mark. I cannot explain it, but a club for whites is different than a club for blacks."

He was right. Maybe he couldn't explain, but he was right and I was wrong. What he couldn't put into words was the connection between mercy and power. In a predominantly white university, in a predominantly white country, with a predominantly white culture, a white boy holds a fist full of aces. Only when blinded by self-interest could the white son of a white engineer fail to see that he had the advantage over the black child of a black laborer.

It's perfectly correct for the powerless to cluster in ways that for the fully empowered would be arrogant, domineering and exclusivist. Mercy is secure enough to grant that without petty, resentful speeches on fairness.

Does this sound like an appeal for affirmative action? Well, it isn't. Mercy can do what laws cannot. I am not speaking to legislation but to attitude. The rich and powerful must show mercy to the weak and impoverished.

Those whom God summons to acts of mercy are the only ones tempted to cry, "Why must *I* always show mercy?" And the answer of heaven is always the same. "Because you have all the aces!"

Modern Christianity in the industrialized world is dangerously close to justifying, even dogmatizing, a callous selfishness that is contrary to the giving, gracious, merciful heart of Jesus. God pleads the case of the oppressed. The Holy Spirit broods up and down the avenues of Western prosperity, calling out to his bride, "Have mercy! Have mercy!"

It would be a terrible thing if we slammed the door on the Holy Ghost, shouting, "Try that line somewhere else. We're conservatives. We go to church, vote Republican, pay our taxes and earn our own way. What we don't do is bleed for the winos and the teenage single mothers and the kids in tenements."

We don't want government programs that play Robin Hood. I don't either. But is there no alternative? Is there no mercy? Should we reform welfare? Yes! But as we do, it is time for the church to show its colors. There are hungry, hurting, illiterate people who need mercy. There are men who need deliverance from one prison or another, little girls who are being preyed upon and old people who cannot pay to heat their homes in winter.

It's the members with deaf ears down at "Marie Antoinette Memorial Church" who will not listen. "Let them eat cake" is the merciless answer of a church that has lost its purpose. Perhaps the governmental gulag of welfare is largely the result of socialism. But maybe part of the blame lies at the door of a merciless and uncaring church.

Some years ago I went to visit an ignorant old farmer

in a large, inner-city hospital. While I waited at the door, a burly nun wrestled him back into the bed she had just changed. I was appalled at her anger. Did she think he enjoyed being an incontinent old man who had to be cleaned up by strange women?

Finally she stormed out, carrying the foul-smelling sheets, and I was able to step in and see my friend. He had tears in his eyes, but a faint smile toyed with his mouth at the sight of me.

"I'll tell you something, Mark," he whispered as he clutched at my hand. "Some of the Sisters of Mercy ain't."

WE GIVE IT BECAUSE WE HAVE IT

When those clearly called to mercy refuse to hear, things go badly in society. As the church goes, so goes the world. If the church is deaf to the cries of the oppressed, why should the government listen for long? Agencies and programs and benefits are drying up in Congress for the very practical reason that we are drowning in debt. The nation cannot afford utopian politics.

By the same token, the church cannot afford a materialistic, self-indulgent consumerism, or to be insensitive to the plight of the poor and oppressed. This is not a liberal and conservative issue. Indeed, the most fiscally responsible must also be the most compassionate and generous. Conservative, activist congregations devoted to welfare reform must be equally devoted to sacrificial servanthood toward hurting humanity.

We must give because we have it, not because we are taxed. We must serve because we have the strength, not because it's good politics in a poor district. We must find the towel we have mislaid and that old basin long left unused, and get back to the business of dirty feet.

This is not rhetoric. This is Christianity!

I have heard lately more talk about revival than ever in my life. I also long for it. But the Word of God is clear: He desires mercy, and not sacrifice (Hosea 6:6).

An unholy, faithless, backslidden, formal church is not pleasing to God. Neither is an excited, turned-on, growing evangelical church with no heart for those who need mercy. We are called to blow a trumpet in Zion, but the melody is not supposed to be Santa Ana's "Degüello."

The price is much of the problem. Mercy is always costly. For someone to receive mercy, someone else must pay the way, pull the load or die on a cross. Time, involvement, embarrassment, money and frustration are but a few among the many expenses of mercy. We know this and we prove that we know it when we studiously avoid missions programs. Something tells us, *This will cost me.*

We wash feet that just get dirty again and again and again. Can't they keep their feet clean? We load grubby little kids into Sunday school buses at trailer parks that seem to keep on sprouting even more grubby little kids. Is there no end to their irresponsibility?

The sheer scope of the oppression and poverty in this present age is daunting enough to keep many bound up in merciless inactivity. Goal-oriented Westerners want to finish the task and say, "Ah, there now, that's done. What's next?" But the slums of Bombay are not going to get "done." Never will all the rural poor of Appalachia be educated. The war zones of inner-city America may never, ever be gunless and drugless. But what does that mean? That because mercy cannot earn us the delight of a finished task, we must show no mercy at all? God forbid!

The Merciful Mexican

Carl and Joan Loflin had made the tedious journey to Washington because they felt very passionate about prayer in public schools. They had tried to get others from their small midwestern congregation to come with them, but somehow Carl and Joan had been unable to energize their church on the Christian issues, even after Pastor Tom had made them the cochairs of the Christian Activism Team. The clever acronym, CAT, had failed to attract much attention, and lately Carl and Joan had begun to feel that Pastor Tom's heart was not really as into these issues as it should have been. This did not surprise them at all, since they had already joined and left a half-dozen churches in town because of just such insensitivity.

At any rate, they were here at long last, and the rally was all they had hoped it would be. Carl and Joan had been particularly blessed by riding out to the suburbs on buses to picket the homes of certain liberal judges. At one house, a mansion in Chevy Chase, the judge's teenage daughter had wept at the sight of the signs. Joan was particularly encouraged by this and explained to Carl that this indicated the girl's heart was still tender to the Lord.

In fact, the only fly in the ointment at the entire rally was the speaker now at the podium. The Loflins had been watching some powerful street theater by a group of teenagers and had missed the introduction. They did not know who he was, and it seemed that no one around did, either.

He was a commanding speaker, to be sure, confident and authoritative, with a powerful voice, but something about him made Joanie uncomfortable right from the start. She told Carl this, and he took it very seriously. Joan had an uncanny discernment in these matters and could often pick up on error long before it became apparent to others. The man was well into his talk when the Loflins really tuned in, but Carl sensed in a few seconds that Joanie's caution flag should not be ignored.

"Once a Pakistani family immigrated to a small midwestern town," the speaker was saying. "They felt lonely and disconnected. This was especially true of their lovely teenage daughter who was out of touch with American youth culture, having been brought up in a very sheltered way."

Where was he going with this? Carl wondered. The only Pakistanis in their town ran the local convenience store. Carl did not like them, and when he had demanded they remove certain magazines from the store, the foreign man had said only that he also despised the magazines but that the owner was an American who would not change the policy. So far this was not a story Carl liked.

"When this girl started going to school, no one was very nice to her. She became very depressed and introverted. One day she fell down the steps at the high school, and no one would help. The president of the school's Christian club wanted to help her, but she was afraid it would compromise her witness to be seen with a Muslim. An outspoken Christian athlete also saw her, and his heart went out to her. But when she fell the girl's skirt had ridden up, and he did not want anyone to think he was peeking, so he quickly went inside."

"I told you!" Joanie said. "Sex and foreigners!"

"I know," Carl responded sharply. "Listen. I want to know *exactly* what he says. I don't want to be accused of misquoting him later when I write to the rally leaders. They should never have let this guy on the platform, and if they haven't figured that out yet I'm going to make it plain."

"A Mexican kid whose father was in jail on drug charges finally came and helped the girl," the speaker continued.

This caused a stir in the crowd. They were growing restless. Who was this speaker and what in the world was he talking about? The rally leaders were also getting nervous. No one seemed to know who the speaker was. Someone signaled the organist, who started the *Battle Hymn of the Republic*. A songleader leapt to another microphone and soon the rally was singing with gusto. Seeing that continuing to speak was useless, the unknown speaker left the platform.

Carl and Joan smiled knowingly at each other and others around them. It was wonderful to be a part of something so powerful. They had shown that speaker they were not a bunch of stupid sheep who could be force-fed such sentimental tripe. Just the sound of fifty thousand committed voices drowning out some idiotic story about Mexicans and Pakistanis, just the sound of it was thrilling! *His truth* is marching on!

Carl decided then and there that he would still write the letter. Even though they had effectively gotten the speaker off the platform, the organizers needed to be reminded they also were being watched. Anybody can make mistakes, but too many of that kind of mistake is what gets leadership replaced. Anyway, Carl *liked* writing letters.

MERCY DOES WHAT IT CAN

I grew up from pillar to post. My dad moved us around like a bunch of barn burners. I grew up on a diet of several schools a year, constant change and an ever-present knowledge that wherever we were, it wasn't permanent. My mother helped me to find a balanced vision that has stood me in good stead.

"Don't make your dream to stay in one house," she

told me. "Instead, determine to leave every new flower bed in better shape than when you found it."

A decade ago I stumbled upon Southeast Asia's dirty little secret: child prostitution. Surely many already knew the terrible story, but it was shocking news to me. One million children live lives of enforced degradation so evil and so demeaning that it boggles the mind. Most, like the girls of Northern Thailand, are sold in squalid tribal villages in the mountains, carried down to urban centers like Bangkok and beaten into submission. There they serve the lusts and perversions of cruel customers who for a pittance prey on these children's bodies like sexual vultures.

Sold at twelve years old and led away weeping at the end of a rope, an Akha girl becomes a hard-eyed prostitute in the brothels of Bangkok before she is thirteen. Seventy-five percent of these girls are HIV-positive. Six or eight men a night and enough beatings and cruelty to break her spirit turn an innocent child into a used-up, AIDS-infected old woman by her nineteenth birthday, when she will be turned out into the street to die.

I cannot rescue a million such children. I cannot end the traffic in little bodies and souls. I cannot stop the planeloads of Japanese and Western businessmen who come to debauch themselves and then go home to their wives. I cannot save every girl in every brothel in Bangkok. But I can save a few.

House of Grace was launched, by the mercies of God, nearly ten years ago. Into its doors have come Akha girls whose lives were about to be wasted by depravity and disease. Out of its doors have come fine young Christian women who have learned to read and write, to pray, to serve and find their destinies. House of Grace is a compound of beautiful buildings filled with the happy, wholesome laughter of innocent little girls playing volleyball and hemming their school uniforms. From its dormitories and playgrounds are graduating young women ready to work as teachers and bookkeepers and nurses.

I have no illusion that I am making much of a dent in the murderous rings of child prostitution in Southeast Asia. They have been and will be a curse in the earth. But I can show mercy to some of their victims.

MERCY MINISTRIES

It is to "show mercy" that we Christians are commanded by Christ himself in Matthew 25. In fact, the ministries of mercy will be, according to that passage, the watershed of eternity, dividing "the sheep from the goats." Jesus lists three specific people groups in need of mercy ministries: refugees, the impoverished and the imprisoned.

There are merciful Christians and churches all over the world determined to meet the challenge of showing mercy. In Rwanda, children of the African holocaust are cared for in Christian orphanages. Inner-city churches feed and clothe the poor on a daily basis. And into the prisons of the world march the brave and the merciful with their Bibles under their arms.

The divine summons to house the homeless, feed the hungry and reach out to the incarcerated is not an invitation to a begrudging surrender to the will of an unreasonable God. In showing mercy, we receive it. "Give and it shall be given unto you." There is a precious mercy for those who show mercy. It is the mercy of meaningful living.

You must, by all means, rejoice in the mercy of God for your salvation. The tender keeping mercies of God that sustain you in your griefs and fears are wonderful. But there is another kind of mercy. It is not an idea or a concept or a theology. It is the fulfillment of giving that is so totally unknown by the voracious consumers of this world.

Through your church, at a soup kitchen, with your checkbook or at a nearby prison, "show" mercy. Refuse to become merely a hearer of the word; act, move and actually *do* it.

Find a nursing home. In it find a single old lady who waits in loneliness for a family that never comes to visit. Visit her. There is a child somewhere waiting to be taught, a mentally retarded girl to be read to or a roof to be repaired. Mercy in you cannot bear the entire weight of the world. But it can learn to laugh again and give again and embrace the whole crazy, dirty world again. Mercy cannot heal all the sick, teach all the untaught and empty all the slums. But it can do something. And it can give you back your sense of humor and your purpose, and rearrange your priorities.

At the height of Germany's terrible air attack on Britain during World War II, a massive bomb penetrated the roof of a hospital but fell impotently to the floor. The bomb squad dismantled the awful device and found to their amazement that the detonator had been left out. In its place was a note written in poor English. Some unknown Czechoslovakian prisoner, working as a slave in a German munitions factory, had assembled the bomb to fail and somehow slipped the note in. It said: *For today, is all I can do.*

Perhaps instead of grinding our own axes, or trying to get our way or win whatever church argument is underway at the moment, maybe we should figure out what we can do today and just do it; and as Paul says in Romans 12:8, show it with cheerfulness. Not all our doctrines nor all our media blitzes combined can make as great an impact on a weary, waiting world as can cheerful mercy shown—actually *shown*—in the love of Jesus Christ.

NOTES

Two
Mercy's Price Tag

1. William Cowper (1731–1800), "There Is a Fountain."
2. Cowper, "There Is a Fountain."
3. Ernest Hemingway, *Islands in the Stream* (New York: Scribner, 1970).
4. C.B. Widmeyer, "Come and Dine."

Three
God's Wide Mercy

1. Frederick W. Faber (1814–63), "There's a Wideness in God's Mercy."

Seven
Keeping Mercies

1. Annie Johnson Flint (1866–1932), "He Giveth More Grace," © 1941, renewed © 1969 Lillenas.